Rosemary Shrager's
School for Cooks

An RDF Media Group production as seen on ITV1

Contents

I am passionate about food and cooking, and I love teaching others to appreciate food and how to cook. I am largely self-taught – I have had no formal training – but I think this has, perhaps strangely, been an advantage. As I have made my tentative way into new cooking techniques and unfamiliar concepts, I learned to understand them better because I was doing it on my own, without anyone guiding me and holding my hand. In a sense I had to learn the hard way, and it was sink or swim. This has possibly made me a better teacher as well...

It all goes back to my childhood, which is when I first began to understand where food came from, and when – for seasonality is still one of my passions. My mother was a good cook and had a kitchen garden that supplied us with vegetables and fruit throughout the seasons. I was barely six years old when I was helping her dig, and it was great fun unearthing the sweet new potatoes in May, and picking runner and French beans throughout the summer. I have such strong "taste" memories, all instilled at that time: munching freshly plucked raspberries (our geese lived among the canes); stuffing myself with baby peas (more in me than in the basket); I even remember the flavour of the top of the milk mixed with a little sugar. This wasn't greed, it was pure pleasure, and something like that never leaves you. We had a cherry orchard too, and

later my parents used to send boxes of cherries to me
at boarding school, which made me rather popular with
the other girls!

My mother encouraged me to cook as well, and I was
entering village fêtes and fairs at the age of eight with my scones
and biscuits. I used to make them look pretty, cutting them
into shapes – stars, circles and rectangles – and I'm still at it all
these years later. Because I went to art college in my late teens, I
learned to love colour, shape, texture and feel, and combinations
of all of these, and this is what I now like to bring to a plate of
food. I want to see a beautiful picture on a plate. However,
flavour is still paramount, of course. If I have a dish involving
puff pastry, the shape of that is important, but the sauce to go
with the fish and pastry will have been chosen to complement
both perfectly, as will the various accompanying vegetables.
I start with the background of my culinary picture, adding the
layers and refinements as I go until there is a rich, woven
togetherness, which I hope will make for a wonderful dish.

However, although there are many elements to my
individual dishes, I don't think that my cooking is complicated.
It is classic, not unusual or innovative, and uses techniques that
are already out there. I have learned on the hoof over a good
30 years, firstly doing directors' lunches, outside catering and
running my own restaurant in Cornwall, then later working

really hard in several top restaurant kitchens, asking questions of chefs and suppliers, watching chefs at work, reading books and making endless notes (my memory is like a sieve). It's been hard work! I also drew pictures, with colours and shapes annotated and labelled. It is these ways of learning that I utilise in my teaching today, based on my own experience.

Teaching cookery is almost as much of a passion for me as are food and cooking themselves. The people I meet, both at my Swinton Park courses and in *School for Cooks*, all share my enthusiasm. They are determined to learn, to succeed, sometimes even to change their lives, and all that takes single-mindedness, dedication and courage. Helping those who feel as strongly as I do about food is incredibly satisfying – and I have eaten some fantastic food too! On the television programmes, only one person can win the coveted prize each time – to work in a Michelin-starred kitchen – but I like to think that the others are not put off by their apparent failure. They will have listened, absorbed, gained confidence, understood the pressures and learned to go that little bit further. And that will take them quite a way towards achieving their goals in the world of food.

At home, there is no reason why you shouldn't go that little bit further as well. Many of the recipes in this book are amalgams of ideas such as you might find on a restaurant plate of food. Individually the ideas are not difficult, but bringing them together to make my perfect picture might seem a little daunting. You might also think that it would take too much time (although many things can be prepared well in advance). But these are recipes for special occasions, and a special occasion requires dedication, time and effort – and I think you will find that it will work out considerably cheaper than eating in a restaurant! And, of course, you don't have to follow the concepts to the letter: you can adopt, adapt, add, perhaps even improve. Make a delicious stew and serve it simply with a potato purée instead of encasing it in a sophisticated wrapping; mix and match the vegetable accompaniments to make a recipe uniquely your own. Cut vegetable garnishes just a little smaller to get nearer to the visual splendour of restaurant dishes; reduce liquids just a few moments longer and put them through a fine sieve to approach the intensity and silkiness of a professional sauce.

It's all about knowledge, practice, self-belief and self-confidence, and I hope that in my cookery courses, my television programmes and in this book I have manage to instil all of those in you. Good luck!

Soups and Starters

T he first course of a meal is important. Your guests will be hungry, but what you offer them should leave them enough room for the next two courses. A starter is the introduction to the joys that are to come, so it must be attractive and, above all, it must be tasty.

There are lots of ideas here – soups, risottos, pasta, fishy things, pâtés and terrines – most of them classic, many with a modern twist. None is too difficult to achieve, and many can be adapted seasonally or to your taste. For instance, the leek and potato soup on p.21 can be eaten without the salmon, but adding this gives the dish a little extra edge. A number of the soups here can also be turned into main-course dishes: the mussel, vegetable and pearl barley soup (p.17), for instance, would be wonderful for lunch, served with crusty bread. But the soup *pièce de résistance*, I feel, is the beetroot consommé (p.18). It may sound complicated, but if you tackle clarifying (simple) a good home-made chicken stock (even simpler), you will have a really sophisticated first course for a dinner party. Served with the wild mushroom ravioli, it becomes very special indeed.

Risotto and pasta starters are delicious when made well. Of course, I recommend that you make your own pasta: for the ravioli that appear here, home-made is crucial (but good fresh pasta ribbons and lasagne can now be bought). Both risottos and pastas are very versatile. Risottos can be served as starters or main courses, or used as an accompaniment or garnish. And if you think that risottos are difficult to accomplish, requiring 40 minutes or so of concentrated stirring, think again. Italian purists might not approve, but you can gently pre-cook a risotto to the *al dente* stage, then just finish it off at the last minute with a burst of gentle heat and some more stock.

I have included quite a lot of fishy starters, as I like that lightness at the beginning of a meal. Some of the fish dishes are raw, which I like very much. There are also several other raw and virtually raw dishes here, including a couple of raw duck starters.

Terrines and pâtés are first-course classics, and there are several useful techniques employed in the recipes here. It all boils down ultimately to what you use to hold the product together when it is turned out, whether gelatine, eggs or simply butter. Once you have grasped the various concepts involved, you can adapt, adopt and improve to your heart's content.

As with any of my recipes, advance preparation is key: if you have the starter ready to go, you can then concentrate on the other courses. Remember that, with starters, small is beautiful, and don't forget that many of these can be served to vegetarian guests, and even doubled in size to make a main course. Better than an omelette...

Mild Spicy Broth with Noodles, Turbot and Prawns

This fresh-tasting soup combines all the good spring vegetable tastes with an eastern slant, introducing ginger and chilli. The noodles make it a little like a Singaporean laksa, and the turbot transforms the soup into a very superior dinner-party starter – or, indeed, a main-course dish for two people.

Serves 4

150g (5½oz) Japanese soba noodles
50g (1¾oz) French beans, ends trimmed
600g (1lb 5oz) turbot fillet, skinned and cut
  into 16 pieces
salt and pepper
1 bunch spring onions, cut into 2-cm
  (1-in) pieces
2 tbsp groundnut oil
1 fresh green chilli, cut into rounds
12 large raw tiger prawns, peeled and
  deveined (keep the shells for the broth)
coriander leaves, to garnish

Mild spicy broth
1 shallot, finely diced
1 small leek, finely diced
1 tbsp olive oil
1 carrot, finely diced
2 celery sticks, finely diced
2 sprigs thyme leaves
2 bay leaves
2cm (¾in) piece fresh root ginger,
  finely sliced
2 garlic cloves, finely sliced
1 fresh red chilli, finely chopped
1 litre (1¾ pints) Chicken Stock (p.206)

First, make the broth. In a large, heavy saucepan, soften the shallot and leek in the olive oil for 3 minutes over medium heat; do not brown. Add the carrot, celery, thyme, bay leaves, ginger, garlic, red chilli and prawn shells – toss them in the oil and sweat for 2 minutes to soften. Add the stock, bring to a simmer and cook for 20 minutes. Strain through a fine sieve and skim off any scum. You will need 800ml (about 1½ pints) for this recipe.

Preheat the oven to 180°C (350°F/Gas 4). Cook the noodles in boiling salted water until *al dente*. Drain and rinse under cold water; set aside. Cook the French beans in a large pan of boiling salted water for 2–3 minutes. Drain and refresh under cold water.

Pour 200ml (7fl oz) of the broth into a baking dish, then add the turbot. Season with salt and pepper, then cover and cook for 3 minutes in the oven.

In a frying pan, soften the spring onion in the groundnut oil for 1 minute over a medium heat, then add the green chilli and prawns. Cook for 2 minutes, tossing all the time.

To serve, gently warm the broth through (including that from the turbot). Put some noodles in each serving bowl, along with the turbot, and arrange the spring onions and prawns on top. Pour in the hot broth and sprinkle with coriander. Serve hot.

Smoky Bacon Vegetable Soup

This soup is simplicity itself, so far as the cooking is concerned, although timing is important. The "art" or "skill" of it lies in the cutting, as everything has to be the same size – and the cubes are quite small! It's all about presentation. If you want to make a vegetarian soup, simply leave out the bacon and up the seasoning.

Serves 6

60g (2oz) butter
100g (3½oz) smoked bacon, cut into 5mm (¼in) cubes
1 small leek, white and very pale green parts only, cut into 5mm (¼in) cubes
1 shallot, cut into 5mm (¼in) cubes
1 carrot, cut into 5mm (¼in) cubes
1 parsnip, cut into 5mm (¼in) cubes
1 small potato, peeled and cut into 5mm (¼in) cubes
1 celery stick, cut into 5mm (¼in) cubes
2 courgettes, cut into 5mm (¼in) cubes

3 tbsp fresh podded peas (or frozen if necessary)
1.5 litres (2¾ pints) Vegetable Stock (p.208) or Chicken Stock (p.206)
salt and pepper
2 tbsp chopped flat-leaf parsley, plus extra, to garnish
130ml (4½fl oz) crème fraîche
2 Gem lettuces, stalks removed and leaves shredded
2 tomatoes, skinned (p.146), deseeded and chopped

In a large pan, melt the butter and soften the bacon, leek and shallot for 2 minutes over a low heat. Then add the carrot, parsnip, potato and celery and cook for a further 5 minutes. Now add the courgettes, peas and stock, season with a little salt and pepper and cook for 5 minutes.

Next add the chopped parsley, crème fraîche, lettuce and tomato, and cook for a further 1 minute. Serve immediately, garnished with extra parsley.

Mussel, Vegetable and Pearl Barley Soup

On the programme, we were unable to get mussels for this recipe, so we substituted baby squid on the day. Although that worked well, I would always recommend using the original recipe with mussels.

Serves 4

1.5 kg (3lb 3oz) fresh mussels
olive oil
2 garlic cloves, chopped
1 bay leaf
sprig thyme
40g (1¼oz) carrots, finely diced
40g (1¼oz) leek, finely diced
40g (1¼oz) celery, finely diced

250g (9oz) waxy potatoes (such as Désirée), peeled and diced
100g (3½oz) pearl barley
at least 800ml (1½ pints) Vegetable Stock (p.208), Chicken Stock (p.206) or Fish Stock (p.208)
salt and pepper
1 tbsp chopped flat-leaf parsley

First scrub the mussels and remove their beards (see tip below).

Heat 3 tbsp olive oil in a large frying pan with a lid, then add the garlic, bay leaf, thyme and mussels. Cover the pan and cook over a high heat until the mussels have all opened. Discard any that do not open. Remove the opened mussels from their shells, and chop a quarter of them. Keep and filter the mussel cooking liquid through muslin into a bowl or pan.

Soften the carrots, leek and celery in 2 tbsp olive oil in a saucepan for about 5 minutes over a low heat, then add the potatoes, chopped mussels, pearl barley and stock, along with the strained cooking liquid from the mussels. Cover and simmer gently for 45 minutes.

Add the whole mussels and cook for a further 2 minutes. Taste and season with salt and pepper as needed. Serve the soup hot in bowls, sprinkled with the chopped parsley. If you like, drizzle a little very good olive oil on top.

TIP:

Make sure your mussels are as fresh as can be. They should have hard, rounded shells, and you must throw away any that are broken. Scrub your mussels under cold running water and scrape off any barnacles with a small knife. Pull away the stringy "beard" from the mussels (this is how they cling to rocks and ropes). If any mussels continue to gape and do not close when tapped, discard them, as they are probably dead. Similarly, once the mussels are cooked, if they have not opened, they will have died before cooking and should be discarded.

Beetroot Consommé with Wild Mushroom Ravioli

This consommé is absolutely delicious, as rich and earthy in flavour as it is in colour – which is bright red! You could serve it by itself, or perhaps with a good bread (pp.192–98). With some little ravioli floating in it, however, it's elegant, more filling and tasty, and perfect for an autumn dinner-party starter. It takes a bit of time to prepare, I must admit, but can be made the day before. When reheating, *never* boil the consommé, as this will bring scum to the crystal-clear surface.

Serves 6

500g (1lb 2oz) raw beetroot, roughly grated
1 small carrot, roughly chopped
½ leek, roughly chopped
1 celery stick, roughly chopped
2 tomatoes, roughly chopped
3 sprigs dill
1 skinless chicken breast, about 150g (5½oz), roughly diced
6 egg whites
1.5 litres (2¾ pints) cold fresh Chicken Stock (p.206)
salt and pepper

Wild mushroom ravioli
1 quantity pasta for ravioli (p.215), but made with 4 egg yolks and 2–3 tsp each of water and olive oil
10g (¼oz) dried ceps
1 tbsp olive oil
40g (1¼oz) chestnut mushrooms, finely chopped
1 tsp thyme leaves
50g (1¾oz) ricotta cheese

First, make the pasta dough as described on p.215 and chill.

Pureé the beetroot, carrot, leek, celery, tomatoes, dill and chicken in a processor until well blended. Tip the purée into a large pan and add the egg whites and stock. Bring slowly to the boil, stirring all the time. When the first bubbles appear, reduce the heat and stop stirring. Simmer slowly for 1 hour, then remove from the heat. Set aside for 30 minutes.

In the meantime, start the mushroom filling for the ravioli. Pour over enough boiling water to just cover the ceps in a small bowl and set aside for about 30 minutes. Drain the soaked ceps, reserving the liquid, and finely chop.

Heat the oil in a sauté pan and fry the ceps, chestnut mushrooms and thyme over a low heat for a few minutes until just tender. Strain the reserved ceps liquid through a fine sieve into the mushroom mixture in the pan, and continue to cook until the mixture is completely dry. Season well with salt and pepper and leave to cool. When cooled, purée in a blender. Mix the mushroom mixture with the ricotta and adjust the seasoning as needed. Make the ravioli as described on p.215, with the mushroom and ricotta mixture. Place on a floured baking tray, cover and refrigerate until needed.

Pass the beetroot consommé through a fine sieve lined with muslin, set over a clean pan. Be careful not to press or move the vegetables too much, or the liquid will become cloudy. Warm the clear red liquid through gently and check the seasoning.

Meanwhile, bring a separate, large pan of salted water to the boil; cook the ravioli for 1–2 minutes until *al dente*. Drain carefully, removing the ravioli with a slotted spoon.

To serve, ladle the warm beetroot consommé into serving bowls. Add three to five ravioli per bowl, season with salt and pepper and serve.

Leek and Potato Soup with Confit of Organic Salmon

This flavourful soup is lovely by itself, perfect as a lunch dish simply served with crusty bread. But with a small portion of briefly cooked salmon floating in it, it becomes something much more special. To "confit" something means to cook it in oil. This technique may seem unhealthy, but it's not at all. If you are not convinced, you can simply steam the salmon.

Serves 4

350g (12oz) cleaned and trimmed leeks, white and pale green parts only, chopped into small pieces
2 garlic cloves, chopped
60g (2oz) butter
250g (9oz) floury potatoes (such as Maris Piper or King Edward), peeled and diced
500ml (16fl oz) Chicken Stock (p.206)
300ml (10 fl oz) milk
salt and pepper
100ml (3½fl oz) double cream

Confit of salmon
olive oil
1 tbsp thyme leaves
2 garlic cloves
400g (14oz) organic salmon, skin off, cut into 4 pieces

To garnish
coarse sea salt
6 sprigs chervil
2 tbsp finely snipped chives

In a large pan, soften the leek and garlic in the butter for about 5 minutes over a low heat. Now add the potato, stock and milk. Bring to the boil, reduce the heat slightly and simmer for about 40 minutes. Remove from the heat and allow to cool for 10 minutes, then transfer to a blender and purée (or use a hand-held blender, if you prefer). Pass the mixture through a fine sieve into a clean pan. Season well with salt and pepper and add the cream to finish. Keep to one side until needed.

When ready to cook the salmon, first heat enough olive oil to cover the fish to 60°C (140°F), along with the thyme and garlic. Put in the salmon pieces and cook gently for 7 minutes, but check after 5 minutes to see if there are any white bubbles (this is the protein coming out of the fish), which indicate that the fish is done. Remove the salmon from the oil using a slotted spoon and rest on kitchen paper for 5 minutes.

To serve, heat the soup through. Put a piece of salmon in each soup bowl, surround with the soup and add the garnish – coarse sea salt and chervil on the salmon and chives on the soup.

Artichoke and Herb Risotto

I love to use globe artichokes when they are in season. They are delicious served simply boiled, with melted butter or vinaigrette, or you can denude the vegetable and serve the heart or bottom in a number of different ways. Here, we use diced artichoke to flavour a risotto, and this risotto, although good by itself, is wonderful as the base for a loin of rabbit stuffed with, yes, some more artichoke (pp.115–17).

Serves 4

4 globe artichokes
1 litre (1¾ pints) Vegetable Stock (p.208) or Chicken Stock (p.206)
4 tbsp olive oil
100g (3½oz) unsalted butter
1 small red onion, finely chopped
1 garlic clove, finely chopped
250g (9oz) risotto rice

100ml (3½fl oz) dry vermouth or "hot wine"
4 tbsp chopped herbs (such as tarragon and flat-leaf parsley)
50g (1¾oz) Parmesan cheese, freshly grated
4 tbsp double cream
salt and pepper

Cook the artichokes in boiling water for 25 minutes. Remove from the water using a slotted spoon and allow to cool. Once cooled, remove all the leaves and scoop out the thistle-like fibres, or choke, from the centre of the artichokes using a teaspoon. Cut the artichoke bottoms into 1cm (½in) dice.

Heat the stock to a simmer in a large heavy pan, then keep hot.

Heat the oil and half of the butter in a separate large pan, and soften the onion over a medium heat for 2–3 minutes without allowing it to colour. Stir in the garlic and cook for about 2 minutes, stirring gently with a wooden spoon from time to time. Add the rice and stir until all the grains are well coated in fat, allowing to cook for 1–2 minutes. Add the hot wine and wait until this is fully absorbed by the rice before you start adding the stock. Add the hot stock to the rice ladle by ladle, stirring gently; wait for each ladleful of liquid to be absorbed before adding another. The risotto is ready when almost all the liquid has been absorbed and the grains are soft, but still have a "bite". This should take about 25 minutes.

When the risotto is ready, add the artichoke dice and, just before serving, stir in the herbs, Parmesan, the remaining butter and the cream. Season with salt and pepper to taste.

Roasted Red Pepper Risotto

Roasted peppers are good in salads by themselves or with other vegetables, and are traditionally served as an antipasto in Italy. They are also useful in other dishes, such as this risotto. It serves as a good starter with some grated or shaved Parmesan on top, but it also makes an ideal base for grilled or fried meat or fish, especially the red mullet on pp.60–61 (when you would use fish rather than chicken stock).

Serves 4

1 tsp saffron threads
150ml (5fl oz) white wine
1 litre (1¾ pints) Fish Stock (p.208) or
   Chicken Stock (p.206)
2 red peppers
2 tbsp olive oil
2 shallots, finely chopped
1 leek, finely chopped
250g (9oz) risotto rice

4 tbsp double cream
25g (scant 1oz) unsalted butter, chilled
   and diced
1 tbsp finely snipped chives
salt and pepper

Parmesan Crisps
100g (3½oz) Parmesan cheese, freshly and
   finely grated

Preheat the oven to 180°C (350°F/Gas 4).

Make the Parmesan crisps first. Place a pastry cutter on a non-stick baking tray and sprinkle some of the Parmesan inside in a thin layer. Gently remove the cutter and repeat to make more Parmesan circles. Place in the oven for 4–5 minutes until the cheese is melted and golden. Working quickly, remove the tray from the oven and lift each disc off onto non-stick paper. You can leave them as rounds or immediately twist into a shape of choice. Within seconds the Parmesan will crisp up. Leave to one side.

Put the saffron and white wine in a small pan and simmer over a high heat for 2 minutes. Remove from the heat and set aside to infuse for 20–30 minutes. Bring the fish stock to a simmer in a medium pan, then keep hot.

Preheat the grill to high and grill the peppers, turning occasionally, until well blackened and blistering all over. Put the peppers in a bowl, cover with cling film and set aside for 10–15 minutes. Peel off the skin: it should come away easily. Cut the peppers in half, remove and discard the seeds, then cut the flesh into fine dice. Keep to one side.

Meanwhile, heat the oil in a large heavy pan and soften the shallots and leek over a medium heat for 2–3 minutes without colouring. Add the rice and cook as described opposite, adding the infused wine and saffron followed by the stock.

When the risotto is ready, carefully stir in the diced red pepper, followed by the cream, butter and chives. Season with salt and pepper.

Cream Cheese Bavarois with Confit of Baby Fennel and Asparagus

This is a nice summery starter, using the young new season's asparagus and baby fennel. A bavarois is usually cream- and custard-based, and I have used the name here because of the creamy cheese base. It's a very quick and easy dish.

Serves 4

1 gelatine leaf
juice of ½ lemon
250g (9oz) good cream cheese
  (from a packet if you like)
150ml (5fl oz) whipping cream
pinch of cayenne pepper
salt and white pepper

Confit of fennel and asparagus
12 asparagus spears
100ml (3½fl oz) extra virgin olive oil

4 baby fennel bulbs
juice of ½ lemon
2 bay leaves
2 sprigs of tarragon leaves

To garnish
2 ripe tomatoes, skinned (p.146), seeded
  and finely diced
1 tbsp finely chopped dill
1 tbsp finely snipped chives

First soak the gelatine in cold water for 15 minutes. In a small saucepan, heat the lemon juice. Squeeze the excess liquid out of the softened gelatine leaf, add to the lemon and stir until completely melted.

Soften the cream cheese by whisking it lightly. Lightly whisk the whipping cream, and fold into the cream cheese. Add a pinch each of cayenne, salt and white pepper, then fold in the melted gelatine. Divide the mixture among four small dariole moulds (you might have enough for six) and put into the refrigerator for 3 hours or until set.

To prepare the asparagus, lightly peel the stems, then put the spears in boiling salted water for 1–2 minutes. Drain well and dress with the extra virgin olive oil while still warm. Cut the fennel bulb into quarters lengthways and blanch in simmering water for 3 minutes or until tender. Drain well and add to the asparagus and olive oil while still warm. Now add the lemon juice, bay leaves and tarragon leaves and carefully mix so everything is well coated with the flavours. Season well with salt and pepper and leave at room temperature.

To serve, turn out the cream cheese bavarois onto individual serving plates and arrange the drained fennel and asparagus around (reserve the oil for another time). Garnish the plate with the diced tomato, chopped dill and chives.

Twice-baked Goat's Cheese Soufflé with Salsa and Pesto

For this, you need a good cheese that will melt well: a plain creamy goat's cheese, an ordinary French one or something local. This is such a good recipe for entertaining, as you can cook it in advance and reheat at the last minute. You could even freeze the little soufflés after the first cooking, then thaw and reheat.

Serves 4

60g (2oz) unsalted butter
30g (1oz) plain flour
150ml (5fl oz) milk
salt and pepper
3 tbsp goat's cheese
3 tbsp freshly grated Parmesan cheese
2 large egg yolks
pinch of cayenne pepper

salt and pepper
4 large egg whites

To serve
1 quantity Warm Yellow and Red Pepper Salsa (p.218)
1 quantity Fresh Herb Pesto (p.218)

Make the béchamel base first by melting half of the butter in a small saucepan over a low heat. Add the flour and cook for 1 minute, being careful not to brown the roux. Boil the milk and gradually add to the roux, stirring continuously with a wooden spoon. Beat well and heat until the sauce thickens, then reduce the heat and cook for a further 2 minutes. Remove the pan from the heat and cool slightly.

Spoon the béchamel into a bowl and mix in the grated goat's cheese and 2 tbsp of the Parmesan. Leave to cool. Add the egg yolks and beat until smooth. Season with cayenne and salt and pepper to taste.

Preheat the oven to 190°C (375°F/Gas 5). Use half of the remaining butter to grease four 8cm (3¼in) ramekins well. Coat the inside of each one with the remaining Parmesan. Place on a baking tray in the refrigerator until required.

In a stainless-steel or ceramic bowl, whisk the egg whites until they reach the soft peak stage. Fold one-third of the egg whites into the goat's cheese mixture to slacken it, then fold in the remainder. Fill the ramekins to the top with the mixture. Smooth the tops and run your thumb around each ramekin, just inside the rim (this helps rising). Put the tray with the ramekins in the oven and cook for 15 minutes.

While the soufflés cook, butter four little gratin dishes (or one large one, if you prefer). Take the ramekins out of the oven and turn out each soufflé onto a gratin dish. Pop them back into the oven for 10 minutes. Remove from the oven and serve immediately surrounded with the salsa and pesto.

Pancetta and Asparagus with Tomato Compôte and Goat's Cheese Ravioli

When asparagus is in season, I like to make the most of it, serving it in many ways. (There's nothing to beat it simply boiled or steamed with melted butter.) This is slightly more elaborate, and of course the asparagus in pancetta can be served by itself, with a little tomato compôte (a useful little recipe, as it can be made in advance). It is wonderful, though, with a few little ravioli on the side.

Serves 4

8 asparagus spears
8 slices pancetta
100ml (3½ fl oz) olive oil
finely grated zest and juice of ½ lemon
salt and pepper
handful of basil leaves

Goat's cheese ravioli
1 quantity pasta for ravioli (p.215)
200g (7oz) spinach, stalks removed
60g (2oz) butter
100g (3½ oz) goat's cheese
5 tbsp chopped flat-leaf parsley
2 tbsp chopped basil
olive oil

Tomato compôte
2 tbsp olive oil
1 shallot, finely chopped
2 garlic cloves, finely chopped
½ small, fresh red chilli, deseeded and finely chopped
300g (10oz) ripe tomatoes, skinned (p.146), deseeded and chopped
1 tsp caster sugar
200ml (7fl oz) Chicken Stock (p.206) or Vegetable Stock (p.208)
2 tbsp balsamic vinegar

First, make the ravioli pasta dough, as described on p.215. Leave the dough to rest while you make the filling.

Wilt the spinach in a large pan of boiling water with the butter, and drain very well. Squeeze the final bit of liquid out in a clean tea towel, as the spinach must be dry. Season well with salt and pepper, and chop finely. Put the spinach in a bowl, add the goat's cheese, chopped parsley and basil, and mix well; if you feel it needs a final blend, give it a whiz in a food processor or blender. Season well with salt and pepper. Chill.

Make the ravioli as described on p.215. Cook in a large pan of boiling salted water for 2 minutes until *al dente*. Drain carefully with a slotted spoon and transfer to a bowl with some olive oil so that they don't stick together. Set aside until ready to heat through.

To make the compôte, heat the olive oil in a pan over a medium heat and cook the shallot until soft but not coloured, about 2 minutes. Add the garlic and chilli, and cook for a further minute. Add the tomatoes, sugar, stock and balsamic vinegar, and simmer gently until all the liquid has evaporated. Season with salt and pepper and keep warm.

Trim any woody parts from the stems of the asparagus, and wrap each spear in a slice of pancetta. Heat half of the oil in a frying pan over a medium-high heat and quickly fry the asparagus wrapped in pancetta until crisp and golden.

Mix the remaining olive oil with the lemon juice and zest to make a dressing, and season with salt and pepper.

To serve, toss the ravioli with the compôte and arrange the asparagus wrapped in pancetta on top. Drizzle the dressing around and garnish with the basil leaves.

Pumpkin and Sage Ravioli with a Pumpkin and Sage Sauce, Garnished with Sage Crisps

In autumn, when pumpkins are at their glorious best, this would make a splendid dinner-party starter – or indeed a great lunch dish. You can also use butternut squash instead of the pumpkin, which is available all year round.

Serves 4

Pumpkin and sage ravioli
1 quantity pasta for ravioli (p.215), flavoured with a pinch of saffron threads boiled in the water
450g (1lb) pumpkin flesh
50g (1¾oz) ricotta cheese, well drained
1 tbsp finely chopped sage
salt and pepper
2 tbsp freshly grated Parmesan cheese
1 egg yolk
1 tsp caster sugar

Pumpkin sauce
15g finely diced shallots
1 small garlic clove, finely chopped
30g (1oz) butter
150g (5oz) pumpkin flesh, cut into 1cm (½in) dice
200ml (7fl oz) Sauternes or other sweet white wine
250ml (8fl oz) Vegetable Stock (p.208) or Chicken Stock (p.206)
50ml (1¾fl oz) double cream
pinch of cayenne pepper

To garnish
deep-fried sage (see tip opposite)

Make the pasta dough and, while it is resting, start the filling. Preheat the oven to 180°C (350°F/Gas 4). Cut the pumpkin in half, remove the seeds and cut the flesh into 3cm (1¼in) slices. Put on a baking tray and roast for about 1 hour until soft.

Remove the pumpkin from the oven and allow to cool. Dry well. Purée the flesh in a blender or food processor until smooth. Put in a non-stick pan and quickly dry off the liquid on the hob if required, but being careful not to brown the pumpkin. The idea is to have the pumpkin as dry as possible. Allow to cool again.

In a large bowl, mix the puréed pumpkin, ricotta and chopped sage, and season well with salt and pepper. Stir in the Parmesan, egg yolk and sugar. Use this filling to make the ravioli as on p.215. Keep to one side.

To make the sauce, soften the shallot and garlic in the butter in a large frying pan over a low heat. Add the pumpkin and soften gently for 5 minutes. Remove the contents of the pan to a plate or bowl and deglaze the pan with the Sauternes for 5 minutes, using a wooden spoon to scrape up any bits on the bottom of the pan. Return the pumpkin mixture to the pan. Add the stock and cook for 15–20 minutes until the liquid has reduced by half and the pumpkin softened.

Pour the pumpkin mixture into a fine sieve set over a pan to catch the liquid. Purée half of the sieved pumpkin pieces until smooth and add to the liquid to thicken. Repeat with a little more pumpkin if necessary, until you have the right consistency – a medium creamy sauce. Don't worry if there is a little pumpkin left over. Finally, add the cream and season well with cayenne, salt and pepper. Keep warm until needed.

Put a large pan of salted water on to boil, reduce the heat to a simmer, then add the ravioli. Simmer for 3 minutes until *al dente*. Carefully drain the ravioli with a slotted spoon and add to the pumpkin sauce. Toss well, and top with the deep-fried sage.

TIP:

Deep-fried sage leaves make a great garnish for a number of dishes. Choose good, large sage leaves (two per person usually). Deep-fry them in hot sunflower oil until crisp – this will take only moments. Drain well on kitchen paper.

Mint can also be deep-fried in the same way as a dessert garnish.

Tuna and Prawn Salade Niçoise

Salade niçoise is a traditional Provençal dish, which is delicious, but here I have added a few ideas to give it a modern twist. It makes for a decorative first course, and you can make it look exceedingly pretty when arranged on a big platter or individual dishes. You don't have to include the prawns.

Serves 4

75g (2½oz) fine green beans, trimmed
olive oil
1 garlic clove, crushed
salt and pepper
12 new potatoes (such as Charlotte or
  Jersey Royal), peeled
1 fresh tuna fillet, about 400g (14oz)
4 raw tiger prawns
8 quail's eggs, soft-boiled
12 cherry tomatoes, halved

basil-infused olive oil (p.46)
small handful of basil leaves
small handful of rocket leaves
handful of stoned black olives

Tapenade croûtons
4 slices French loaf
olive oil
4 tbsp tapenade

Blanch the beans in rapidly boiling water for 3–5 minutes, then drain. While still warm, add a little olive oil and the garlic, season with salt and pepper, and toss. Boil the potatoes until tender, then cut in half and toss in olive oil and salt in another bowl.

Using a ridged cast-iron grill pan, sear the tuna in a little hot olive oil on each side for 2 minutes, then cut into thin vertical slices and set aside. Fry the prawns in the same pan and oil until they change colour and are no longer opaque. Soft-boil the quail's eggs for 2 minutes, then plunge into iced water. Leave everything to cool a little.

To make the croûtons, preheat the oven to 180°C (350°C/Gas 4). Brush both sides of the bread with a little oil and place on a baking sheet. Bake in the oven for 6–7 minutes. When the croûtons have cooled slightly, spread with the tapenade.

To assemble, arrange a pile of beans on each plate with six tomato halves, one tapenade croûton, two shelled quail's eggs (do this shelling *very* carefully), six potato halves, one prawn and a quarter of the tuna. Drizzle with basil oil. Garnish with the basil and rocket leaves and the black olives.

TIP:

The quail's eggs can be soft-boiled (2 minutes in boiling water) and very carefully shelled in advance. Place in iced water. Just before serving, use a slotted spoon to lower the quail's eggs into simmering water to heat through.

Tuna with Tomato Salsa and a Chicory and Mooli Salad

Like the salade niçoise on pp.30–31, this dish uses virtually raw tuna. The underlying influence here, however, is more oriental in emphasis, with the intense flavour of coriander and a kick from the chilli. Mooli is a kind of Japanese radish.

Serves 4

1 fresh tuna fillet, about 400g (14 oz)
juice of 1 lime
3 tbsp olive oil
salt and pepper

Salsa
1 lime, peeled
½ fresh hot red chilli, deseeded
   and chopped
1 large tomato, skinned (p.146), deseeded
   and chopped

handful of coriander leaves, chopped
3 tbsp olive oil

Chicory and mooli salad
1 head chicory, thinly sliced
5cm (2in) chunk of mooli (daikon or
   Japanese radish), peeled and cut into
   matchsticks
3 tbsp olive oil
1 tbsp white balsamic vinegar
handful of coriander leaves

Marinate the tuna for 1 hour in the lime juice, oil and salt and pepper to taste, then sear all over in a very hot, ridged cast-iron grill pan for a couple of minutes on each side. Chill in the freezer until firm, then slice very thinly.

Segment the lime for the salsa, and chop the segments into small pieces, making sure to catch all the juices. Mix the lime and any juices with the other salsa ingredients.

Put the chicory and mooli in a bowl. Mix together the oil, vinegar and some salt and pepper, and toss the chicory and mooli with this dressing.

To serve, divide the tuna between four plates, and place a quarter of the salad in the middle. Put small spoonfuls of salsa on each slice of tuna and decorate with extra coriander.

Smoked Haddock Gratin

A simple little gratin, with the added advantage that you can prepare it in advance (see the tip below). It's a lovely creamy dish, perfect for a winter supper or starter – what I would call real comfort food.

Serves 6

500g (1lb 2oz) undyed smoked haddock fillet
500ml (16fl oz) full-fat milk
60g (2oz) unsalted butter
300g (10oz) leeks, white part only, cut into
    small cubes

60g (2oz) plain flour
salt and white pepper
pinch of cayenne pepper
100ml (3½fl oz) double cream
150g (5½oz) Cheddar cheese, finely grated

Put the haddock in a pan and cover with some of the milk. Add a little butter and poach over a medium heat for about 5 minutes. Once cooked, keep the milk for the roux. Remove the haddock from the milk and set aside to rest. Drain off the excess liquid and add this to the reserved milk. Remove and discard the bones and any skin from the haddock and flake the flesh.

In a clean saucepan soften the leek in the remaining butter over a very low heat, taking care not to brown it. This can take up to 20 minutes.

Preheat the grill until hot. Add the flour to the softened leek, and cook gently for 30 seconds. Pour in the reserved milk from the haddock, stirring the sauce with a wooden spoon until thick. Continue cooking for a few minutes, then add the flaked haddock. Season well with salt and white pepper, adding the pinch of cayenne.

Put the mixture into six individual ramekins. Add about 1 tbsp of cream on top of each one, then sprinkle with the Cheddar cheese. Put under the hot grill for 1 minute to brown. Serve immediately.

TIP:

Once you have put the haddock mixture in the ramekins, you can place them in the refrigerator and finish the cooking the next day, if you wish. Remove the ramekins from the refrigerator when you are ready to cook, and heat them through in a preheated oven at 190°C (375°F/Gas 5) for 15 minutes. You then top them with the cream and cheese, and brown under the grill as above.

Steamed Squid with Basil Mayonnaise and Tomato and French Bean Salad

This is a wonderful summer first course, or it could be served as a simple salad lunch. I think squid is underrated, possibly because it is almost always cooked wrongly. Cooked for too long, it becomes rubbery; cooked until just tender, it melts in the mouth. Much of this recipe can be prepared in advance, but make sure you assemble it all at the last moment.

Serves 4

400g (14oz) baby squid
salt and pepper
1 quantity Basil Mayonnaise (p.217)

Tomato and French bean salad
150g (5½oz) very fine green beans

4 tbsp best-quality extra virgin olive oil
1 garlic clove
12 small vine tomatoes, skinned (p.146) and halved
squeeze of lemon juice

Clean the squid. Remove the clear backbone from the body, and wash inside the body. Cut the tentacles off just in front of the head and remove the hard bits at the top of the tentacles. Wash the tentacles, too, keeping them whole. Cut the body into rings.

For the salad, top and tail the beans and blanch them in boiling water for 3–4 minutes until just tender. Drain the beans well and put them in a bowl. While they are still warm, cover with half of the olive oil, season well with lots of black pepper and grate the garlic clove over the top. Mix well and allow to cool.

Arrange the beans on the plate with the tomatoes, and drizzle over the remaining oil and some lemon juice. Sprinkle with a little salt just before serving – not before, as the tomatoes will go soggy and exude a lot of liquid.

Season the squid with salt and pepper and steam it for 2–3 minutes until it becomes opaque. Serve with the salad and the basil mayonnaise as an accompaniment.

Carpaccio of Scallops with Pears in Parma Ham

A very simple first course that is especially useful if you don't have much time, this dish must be brought together at the very last minute. The main thing to remember is to use ultra fresh, hand-dived scallops (never those atrocities kept in brine). The roes, if there are any, are not used in this dish, but you can use them in terrines or other dishes, and they can be frozen, too, for using at another time.

Serves 4

8 very fresh large scallops (see tip below)
juice of ½ lemon
olive oil
salt and pepper
2 ripe pears, any variety

6 slices Parma ham
2 handfuls of rocket leaves
1 quantity Parmesan crisps (p.23), curled
  into cigar shapes, to garnish

Clean and thinly slice the scallops widthways and keep to one side.

Mix together the lemon juice and 2 tbsp olive oil, and season lightly with salt and pepper. Set aside.

Peel, core and slice each pear into six. Divide each slice of ham into two, lengthways, and roll a portion of ham around each pear piece. Sear join-side down (to seal) in olive oil in a frying or sauté pan over a very high heat.

Divide the rocket leaves into four portions. Mix the scallops with the lemon juice mixture and season with salt and pepper. Arrange the pears and the scallops over the leaves and garnish with the Parmesan crisps.

TIP:

Put the scallops in the freezer for an hour after they have been cleaned and removed from their shells; this will make them easier to slice. See p.58 for how to remove scallops from their shells.

Escabeche of Red Mullet and Aubergine

Escabeche is the name applied in Spain and Portugal to fish preserved or marinated in vinegar or vinaigrette. Also known as "caveach" in Britain, the technique is found all over the world, from Italy and Africa, through India and across the Pacific to South America. I like it best made with oily fish because it is much richer. When entertaining, this dish makes a great starter because it *has* to be made in advance.

Serves 4

450g (1lb) red mullet fillet, scaled
salt and pepper
olive oil
3 tbsp plain flour
2 tbsp chopped flat-leaf parsley, to garnish

Vegetable marinade
½ aubergine, cut in 5mm (¼in) cubes
½ fennel bulb, thinly sliced
1 carrot, thinly sliced

2 shallots, thinly sliced
2 garlic cloves, crushed
1 tsp coriander seeds, crushed
1 tsp cumin seeds, crushed
150ml (5fl oz) extra virgin olive oil
3 tbsp white wine vinegar
juice of 1 orange
large pinch of saffron threads
1 tsp caster sugar

To make the marinade, sprinkle the aubergine with salt and leave for 30 minutes. Rinse well with cold water and pat dry with kitchen paper. Heat 3 tbsp olive oil in a non-stick or non-reactive pan (with a lid) over quite a high heat, then cook the aubergine cubes, uncovered, for about 5 minutes until very lightly browned. Drain on kitchen paper.

Using the same pan over a low heat, soften the fennel, carrot, shallot, garlic, coriander and cumin in 100ml (3½fl oz) of the extra virgin olive oil for 3 minutes.

Now add the vinegar, orange juice, saffron and sugar, cover with a lid and cook gently for 15 minutes. Remove and allow to cool. Now add the other half of the extra virgin olive oil and the aubergine.

Dust the fish, skin-side only, with flour seasoned with salt and pepper. In a clean frying pan, fry skin-side down in a little olive oil over a medium heat until crisply golden and only just cooked, about 30 seconds.

Place the fish in a dish in one layer in a ceramic or glass serving dish, and pour over the vegetable marinade. Allow to cool. Cover with cling film and put in the refrigerator for as long as possible before serving (at least 2 hours, but preferably overnight).

When you are ready to serve, take the *escabeche* out of the refrigerator, uncover and sprinkle with chopped parsley.

Smoked Salmon and Ginger Terrine with Waldorf Salad

This is a handy recipe when entertaining, as you can make it two to three days in advance. I say it serves 8–10 people, but it would stretch even further, I think. It makes a good starter in the winter, and I have served it at Christmas. It looks very festive, with its green and pink layers.

Makes one 28cm (11in) terrine, to serve 8–10

1 piece smoked salmon, about 800g (1¾lb)
60g (2oz) butter, softened
2cm (¾in) piece fresh root ginger, very finely grated
finely grated zest of 2 limes
juice of 1 lime

1 tbsp chopped dill
1 tbsp chopped flat-leaf parsley
salt and pepper

To serve
1 quantity Waldorf Salad (p.142)

Have ready a narrow 28cm (11in) terrine dish, and line with cling film; leave extra cling film hanging over the sides. Slice the salmon along the top into thin slices, then use enough of the slices to line the terrine's sides and bottom, allowing them to overlap.

Make the butter mixture that holds the terrine together by putting the butter, ginger, lime zest and juice, dill and parsley in a food processor or blender and blitzing until very soft. Season well with salt and pepper.

To assemble the terrine, start by building a layer of the butter mixture in the terrine. Brush this on all over the bottom of the terrine as if you were applying glue or paint. Follow with a slice of salmon. Repeat the brushing on of butter and layering of salmon until you get to the top. Have a final layer of salmon, then fold over the extra cling film to wrap. Chill for at least 4 hours.

Remove the terrine from its dish, then remove the cling film. Serve cut into medium slices, with the Waldorf salad as an accompaniment.

Duck Tartare with Crispy Cabbage and Piquant Vinaigrette

Here is another raw recipe, this time with duck (I do love raw food), but one with a difference. This is my attempt at a little oriental number, using ingredients such as hoisin, mooli, chilli and coriander. I particularly like the deep-fried cabbage, or "seaweed", which, if done well, is absolutely delicious.

Serves 4

Duck tartare
400g (14oz) duck breasts, skinned
1 tbsp hoisin sauce
1 fresh red chilli, deseeded and finely chopped
4 tbsp finely chopped coriander
1 spring onion, finely chopped
salt and pepper

Piquant vinaigrette
3½ tbsp best-quality extra virgin olive oil
juice of 1 lime
1 tbsp hoisin sauce
½ tsp made English mustard (not powder)
5-mm (¼-in) piece fresh root ginger, grated

To serve
2 spring onions
1 quantity crispy cabbage (see Crispy Vegetables, p.127)
4-cm (1¾-in) piece mooli (daikon or Japanese radish), very finely diced
½ red pepper, deseeded and very finely diced
1 tsp soft brown sugar

First make the duck tartare. Trim the duck of all the sinews, and finely dice the meat. Mix with the hoisin sauce, chilli, coriander and spring onion. Season with salt and pepper. Cover with cling film and set aside in the refrigerator.

To prepare the vinaigrette, simply whisk together all the vinaigrette ingredients and pass through a fine sieve. Keep to one side.

Next, slice the spring onion into a fine julienne, place in ice-cold water, cover and refrigerate until needed. Finally, cook the cabbage as described on p.127. This can be done a short time in advance of serving.

To serve, spoon a quarter of the duck tartare into an 8cm (3¼in) cook's ring set on a serving plate. Carefully remove the ring, and top the duck tartare with some crispy cabbage. Repeat for the remaining three servings. Scatter the mooli, red pepper and spring onion garnishes around the tartare, and drizzle the vinaigrette over the vegetables. Sprinkle a pinch of soft brown sugar over each tartare, and serve.

Wild Duck Carpaccio with Celeriac and Orange Vinaigrette

Everyone thinks wild duck should always be cooked, but it can be eaten raw. There are a few provisos: the birds should be freshly shot, preferably fairly young, and should be hung for no longer than a couple of days. The vinaigrette here is delicious. You will use only a small proportion of it in this recipe, but it would work equally well with fish or chicken.

Serves 4

breasts of 2 wild ducks
½ celeriac, peeled
2 tbsp finely chopped basil
4 tbsp extra virgin olive oil
20g (¾oz) Parmesan cheese, freshly shaved

Orange vinaigrette
1 orange, segments only, no juice

2 tsp clear honey
100ml (3½fl oz) extra virgin olive oil
salt and pepper

To garnish
black olives
mizuna leaves

Skin the wild duck breasts, and slice very thinly (see tip below). Keep to one side.

To make the vinaigrette, put the orange segments, honey and oil in a small food processor or blender and blitz. Strain through a fine sieve into a bowl, then season well with salt and pepper. Chill and use within 24 hours.

Slice the celeriac into ribbons on a mandoline, then cut into fine julienne strips. Toss with the vinaigrette (you'll only need about 3 tbsp). Store any leftover vinaigrette in a jar with a tight-fitting lid for another (speedy) use.

Mix the basil and oil and divide between four serving plates. Arrange a quarter of the wild duck on each plate and decorate with the Parmesan shavings. Put a small heap of celeriac beside the duck. Garnish with olives and mizuna leaves.

TIP:

To make the duck breasts easier to slice, put them in the freezer for about 1 hour before slicing. I sometimes sandwich the breast slices between double sheets of cling film and use a rolling pin to bash and flatten them, which also makes them really thin.

Ham Hock, Chicken, Spinach and Wild Mushroom Terrine

Even the title of this dish makes it all sound a bit complicated, and it certainly does take time to prepare – especially as you are using gelatine – but it is worth it. It is served with a tomato chilli jam and a pear and cucumber salad. The finished result looks very pretty indeed and tastes delicious...

Makes one 28cm (11in) terrine, to serve 14–16

Ham hock
1 ham hock, about 1.4kg (3lb)
1 bay leaf
2 sprigs flat-leaf parsley
1 sprig thyme
1 small onion, halved
½ celery stick

Remaining terrine
4 gelatine leaves (8 if you want to serve the terrine on the same day)
300ml (10fl oz) warm Chicken Stock (p.206)
3 skinless chicken breast fillets, about 130g (4¾oz) each
salt and pepper
1 tbsp olive oil
2 shallots, finely chopped
100g (3½oz) wild mushrooms, sliced
300g (10oz) large spinach leaves, to line the terrine
freshly grated nutmeg

Pear and cucumber salad
1 pear, peeled and finely diced
juice of 1 lemon
½ cucumber, peeled, deseeded and finely diced
1 tbsp finely chopped coriander
2 tsp caster sugar

Tomato chilli jam
500g (1lb 2oz) tomatoes, quartered
2 fresh red chillies, seeded and roughly chopped
4 garlic cloves, quartered
4cm (1¾in) piece fresh root ginger, quartered
1 tbsp olive oil
1 tbsp white wine vinegar
2 tbsp hoisin or plum sauce

To serve
cress or other small-leaved garnish herb

Put the ham hock in a large pan with the bay leaf, parsley, thyme, onion and celery. Pour over enough water to cover. Bring to the boil, skimming off any impurities that rise to the surface. Reduce the heat and simmer for about 2½ hours until the meat is falling from the bone. Top up with water throughout cooking to ensure that the hock remains immersed at all times.

Meanwhile, make the tomato chilli jam. Put the tomatoes, chillies, garlic and ginger in a processor and blend until well puréed. Transfer to a large saucepan, add the remaining ingredients and slowly cook for 30–40 minutes until all the liquid has evaporated and the texture is thick and chutney-like. Season to taste, cool and refrigerate until required.

Soak the gelatine in cold water for 10 minutes until soft. Squeeze out any excess water,

and melt the gelatine in 100ml (3½fl oz) of the warm chicken stock. Add the rest of the stock and leave to cool but not set.

Season the chicken breasts with salt and pepper, and steam them for 12–15 minutes, turning them over halfway through the cooking time. When the breasts are cooked, keep warm and cut into thin slices.

In the meantime, heat the oil in a sauté pan and soften the shallots for a few minutes over a low heat. Add the mushrooms, and cook for a few minutes until the mushrooms have softened and all their juices have evaporated. Season with salt and pepper, and allow to cool.

Bring a pan of salted water to the boil and blanch the spinach for 1 minute until just wilted. Drain very well, trying to keep the leaves separate, then dry off on a cloth. Season with a little nutmeg.

Finally, drain the ham hock and, when cool enough to handle, peel off and discard the skin. Take all the meat off the bone and cut into small cubes.

Line a narrow 28cm (11in) terrine with cling film, leaving the excess hanging over the edges. Now line the terrine with the spinach, allowing extra to cover the bottom and sides completely – make sure that there are no gaps. Set aside some of the spinach leaves to cover the top of the terrine.

Put a layer of the ham in the bottom of the terrine, then spoon in a little of the gelatine stock, followed by half of the chicken slices, then add a little more of the gelatine stock. Next, add a layer of mushrooms (use all of them now) and top with the remaining chicken. Finally, finish off with a layer of ham. Remember to season with salt and pepper between each layer, and add the gelatine stock as you go.

Pour the remaining gelatine stock over the terrine to fill, then cover with the remaining spinach. Use the excess cling film to wrap the terrine, then transfer to the refrigerator to chill for several hours until set.

For the salad, toss the pear in a bowl with the lemon juice, then add the cucumber, coriander and sugar. Season well with salt and pepper, and chill until required.

Serve the terrine in slices, accompanied by the tomato chilli jam and pear and cucumber salad, and garnished with herbs.

Chicken Liver Parfait

Both the parfait and the following pâté are delicious on their own, served as a starter with crusty bread. But for a really exciting, extra-special dinner-party dish, why not make both, and serve a slice of one with a small quenelle of the other, along with warm toast and a spoonful of Fresh Mango Pickle (p.219)? It may sound complicated, but all three elements of the dish can be – in fact, need to be – made in advance.

Makes one 28cm (11in) terrine, to serve 8–10

700g (1½lb) chicken livers
1 garlic clove
pinch of five-spice powder
1 egg, plus 1 egg yolk

600ml (1 pint) double cream
1 tbsp brandy
1 tsp salt

Preheat the oven to 150°C (300°F/Gas 2). Line a narrow 28cm (11in) terrine with four large sheets of cling film, allowing it to hang over the sides.

Remove all the sinews from the chicken livers – you should end up with about 550g (1¼lb). Put the livers, garlic, five-spice powder and eggs in a food processor, and purée until smooth. Continue to process while adding the cream. Be careful not to overmix; otherwise the cream will separate. Now, add the brandy and salt. Remove the mixture from the food processor and push through a fine sieve.

Fill the prepared terrine with the chicken liver mixture. Fold the cling film up over the top of the terrine, cover in foil and stand on top of folded newspapers in a small baking tray. Carefully half-fill the baking tray with water and put in the oven for 1 hour 10 minutes. Prod the parfait with a skewer: if the skewer emerges clean and warm, the parfait is ready. Remove the terrine dish from the water and allow the parfait to cool for 12 hours undisturbed.

Take the parfait from the terrine dish, peel off and discard the cling film, and rewrap the parfait in a fresh sheet of cling film. Chill until required – the parfait keeps in the refrigerator for up to a week.

Chicken Liver and Wild Mushroom Pâté

Make the pâté in a bowl, and serve in quenelles (egg or oval shapes). To do this, take two spoons of the same size. Get a rounded spoonful of pâté on one spoon, and mould with the other spoon. Wash the spoons in water between quenelles.

Serves about 8

600g (1lb 5oz) chicken livers
200g (7oz) butter
2 shallots, finely chopped
2 garlic cloves, finely chopped
2 tbsp thyme leaves, chopped

100g (3½oz) wild mushrooms, finely chopped
5 tbsp Cognac
salt and pepper
clarified butter (optional, see tip below)

Remove all the sinews from the chicken livers – you should end up with about 500g (1lb 2oz).

Heat about 20g (¾oz) of the butter in a frying pan over a low heat, and soften the shallots and garlic for 3 minutes – do not allow to colour. Add the thyme and stir through. Next, add the chopped mushrooms and soften for about 5 minutes. Remove the shallot and mushroom mixture from the pan and set aside.

Heat a little more of the butter in the same pan over a medium heat. Cook the chicken livers for 4–5 minutes until soft, a couple of minutes on each side. Remove to a bowl, and deglaze the pan with the Cognac, scraping up any bits from the bottom of the pan with a wooden spoon.

Blend or process the cooked chicken livers with the shallot and mushroom mixture and all the remaining butter, until well blended but still with a fine to coarse texture. Season with salt and pepper, and put in a bowl or individual ramekins. If doing the latter, pour over a very thin layer of clarified butter and chill in the refrigerator to set.

TIP:

To clarify butter, put some butter in a pan and leave it over a very, very low heat, just to melt, so that the residue sinks down to the bottom and clear butter fat comes to the top. Carefully pour off the clear fat into another container, leaving the milk residue at the bottom of the pan. Discard this and use the clarified butter as required.

Chicken à la Grecque with Asparagus, Served with Saffron Lemon Jelly and Wild Rocket

A simple and summery way of cooking chicken. It's delicious combined with asparagus and garnished with cubes of bright yellow jelly. The *pièce de résistance*, though, is the basil oil, which adds intense flavour.

Serves 4

2 chicken legs, skinned, bones removed
extra virgin olive oil
juice of 1 lemon
1 bay leaf
16 asparagus tips
1 small bunch of rocket leaves
basil oil (see tip below)

Saffron lemon jelly
150ml (5fl oz) light Chicken Stock (p.206)
good pinch of saffron threads
2½ gelatine leaves, soaked in cold water
finely grated zest and juice of 2 lemons
salt and pepper

To make the lemon jelly, heat the chicken stock in a saucepan, then add the saffron and soaked gelatine and steep for 15 minutes. Add the lemon zest and juice, and season with salt and pepper to taste. Pour through a fine sieve into a dish about 14 x 11cm (5½ x 4½in) and about 1cm (½in) high) and lined with cling film. Allow to cool. When it is time to serve, cut into small squares: you will need 20–24.

Now you are ready to start the chicken. Cut the chicken into pieces about 1.5cm (¾in) in size. Put in a saucepan with a little oil and gently sauté until cooked. While it is still warm, cover with about 100ml (3½fl oz) of olive oil and the lemon juice, and add the bay leaf. Season well with salt and pepper, and chill until required.

Next, blanch the asparagus in boiling salted water for 1 minute. Drain well and put in with the chicken straight away. Check the seasoning and adjust as needed.

To serve, scatter a few leaves of rocket on four serving plates. Put in five or six little pieces of the chicken on each plate, scatter the asparagus over it, then follow with five or six cubes of the lemon jelly around and a swirl of basil oil.

TIP:

A basil-infused oil makes a delicious garnish for many, mainly summery, dishes and it's very easy to make. Purée the roughly chopped leaves and stalks of a large bunch of basil, then add 150ml (5fl oz) olive oil and blend again. Strain the oil through a fine sieve and pour into a clean jar, cover tightly and store in the refrigerator until needed. It will keep for up to 1 week.

Fish and Seafood

Fish, I feel, is one of those ingredients that frightens a lot of people. They feel that there is too much to do before they can get to the actual cooking stage – all that scaling, gutting, boning and filleting.

All these things are very easy to learn, however, and I teach these techniques in my cookery courses. But if you are really disinclined to learn, or feel that you haven't the time, buy whole fish and get your fishmonger to prepare them for you in the shop. Ask him to give you the bones and all the bits he cuts off. I am always very much in favour of buying the whole product, rather than pieces of fish: for a start, it's cheaper, and you can make a delicious stock to use in soups and sauces with the bones and offcuts (use only the bones of white fish, never those of oily fish). Also, you must always be very certain of the reliability of your supplier and the freshness of your fish. And, remember, fish that has already been frozen – as it might have been, at sea – should never be re-frozen.

To tell whether a fish is fresh, examine it carefully – it must look plump and fresh (rather than dried up), with bright, clear colours; there should be no opacity to the flesh; and the eyes should bulge. Look behind the gills as well: if they are red rather than pink, the fish is fresh. When you are pinboning the fish, if the bones come out with ease, the fish isn't as fresh as it might be. Sniff the fish as well – there should be no smell at all.

Most fish is quite expensive, although you can get hold of trout and salmon fairly economically. It is, however, very good for you, it needs minimal cooking and it can be beautifully presented, making it perfect for special occasions, which is what most of the recipes here are for. Although fish cooking usually involves last-minute work, you can prepare many of the accompaniments ahead of time. With the scallops in puff pastry on pp.56–58, for instance, you can make the pastry box well in advance.

One of the most important things to learn about fish cookery – and cooking in general – is how to adapt. If there's no cod on sale, use another white fish, such as halibut, haddock, John Dory or sea bream. You could prepare the scallop dish (pp.56–58) with prawns instead of scallops. Similarly, the red mullet used in the Red Mullet with Saffron (pp.60–61) could be replaced with mackerel, another oily fish. And, of course, you can endlessly mix and match the vegetable accompaniments and garnishes.

Dressed Crab

Fresh crab is my favourite shellfish: it's sweet, delicious, the yummiest thing ever. I like preparing it, although many might see it as a chore. To me, it's such a lovely thing to do. It's particularly great fun, if you have people staying for the weekend, to have all of you doing it together!

Serves 4

4 live medium crabs, about 450g (1lb) in total
4 tsp mayonnaise (p.217)
squeeze of lemon juice
salt and pepper

1 thick slice white bread
pinch of cayenne pepper
2 medium eggs, hard-boiled
4 tsp finely chopped flat-leaf parsley

Kill the crabs and pick out all the meat as described in the tip below. Keep the white and brown meats in separate piles. Clean the shell well, ready to use later.

Mix the mayonnaise with the white crabmeat. Do not put too much in; it needs to be lightly mixed. Season with a little lemon juice and some salt and pepper. Make breadcrumbs from the sliced bread, then mix into the brown crabmeat. Season well with salt, pepper and cayenne, and another squeeze of lemon. Separate the yolks from the whites of the hard-boiled eggs. Finely chop both, keeping them separate.

To dress the crab, put the white meat on both sides of the shell, with the brown meat in the middle. Now put the chopped egg yolk on one line between the brown and white meat, and the egg white on the other line between the brown and white meat. Going across at an angle, make a fine line with chopped parsley.

Serve with crusty bread and a salad.

TIP:

To kill a crab, turn it on its back and put a metal skewer or the tip of a very sharp knife through its head. Have ready a large saucepan of rapidly boiling water, quickly put in the crabs and cook for 15 minutes per 450g (1lb), then leave a little longer. Remove from the pan and allow to cool.

Once the crab has cooled, take off all the claws, crack them and remove the white meat. Keep to one side. Do the same with the legs, which are much more fiddly. (To be honest, I like to suck the meat from the legs and eat it there and then – cook's perk!) Now, turn the crab head downwards and bash with your fist. This should make it easier to remove the body from the shell. Put your thumb on the head and it should all come away. Discard, along with the dead man's fingers.

Now, remove all the white meat from the body: there's a lot, so be patient and make sure you get into all those crevices. Add to the claw meat. Check for any shell in the meat – it must be completely removed. Next, remove the brown meat from the shell. Lastly, if you want to use it for dressed crab, clean the shell well.

Lobster with Champagne Sauce

People are daunted by the idea of cooking lobsters, but they are so delicious and luxurious that they don't require anything fancy being done to them. The sauce here is simple, plus it can be started in advance and finished off at the last moment.

Serves 4

2 x 600g live lobsters, about 600g
  (1lb 5oz) each
120g (4¼oz) butter, melted
2 tbsp mixed herbs (fresh chives, dill
  and tarragon
salt and white pepper

Champagne sauce
1 shallot, finely sliced
150ml (5fl oz) white wine
175ml (6fl oz) double cream
150ml (5fl oz) champagne

To serve
200g (7oz) fresh fettucine or tagliatelle

Kill and cook the lobsters as described below. Preheat the oven to 220°C (425°F/Gas 7). When the lobsters have cooled, cut them in half lengthways and clean and remove the meat as described below. Clean the inside of the head, and put the meat from the claws and legs into the cleaned head. Brush the meat with lots of butter and sprinkle with herbs. When you are ready to serve, put into the preheated oven for 15 minutes.

To start the sauce, put the shallot into a small saucepan with the wine and reduce to one-third. Add the cream and reduce again to one-third. (You can do all this 2 hours before.) Cook the pasta until *al dente* in boiling salted water. Drain well.

To serve, finish the sauce by bringing the cream up to simmering point and adding the champagne at the last minute. Put the lobster halves onto a plate and put some pasta on the side. Pour the sauce over the lobster.

TIP:

To kill a lobster, cut into the cross on the head that you will see there with a large knife. Then plunge into a large pan of rolling boiling water. Put on the lid and boil for 4 minutes (for a lobster to be cooked again, as in Thermidor) or 5 minutes (for lobster to be eaten as is, in a salad, say). Take out and allow to cool.

When the lobster has cooled, cut it in half lengthways. Remove and discard the stomach sac, then the intestine (a thin black line running down towards a smaller bag in the tail). Remove any coral and the dark-greenish-looking meat known as tomally (the liver), both of which can be used to make pasta sauces. Take out the remaining flesh. Next remove the brain from the head, being careful not to remove the claw knuckles. Finally extract the meat from the claws. Wash the shells if using in the dish.

Scallops in Puff Pastry with Mushrooms and a Madeira Sauce

The look and the taste of this dish are quite unique. You can buy ready-made puff pastry if you want to, but the difference between this and home-made pastry is unbelievable – it's like chalk and cheese.

Serves 4

450g (1lb) puff pastry (p.210)
1 egg yolk, lightly beaten
½ quantity Wild Mushroom Fricassée
8 large scallops, shelled, washed and
   prepared (p.58)
3 tbsp extra virgin olive oil
salt and pepper
1 tbsp chopped chives

handful of tarragon leaves
2 tomatoes, skinned (p.146) and finely diced

Madeira sauce
1 shallot, peeled and chopped
100ml (3½fl oz) Madeira wine
250ml (8fl oz) Fish Stock (p.208)
150ml (5fl oz) double cream

Preheat the oven to 200°C (400°F/Gas 6). Roll out the pastry to a 1cm (½in) thickness, then cut it into four neat rectangles. Using a small sharp knife, cut a line inside each one of the rectangles of pastry about 1cm (½in) from the edge, looking rather like a picture frame, but taking care not to cut all the way through the pastry. Put the rectangles of pastry on a baking tray and brush the top edges with the egg yolk, making sure that you do not brush over the edges or the pastry will not rise evenly. Bake in the oven for 15–20 minutes until golden brown.

Remove from the oven and, while the pastry is still hot, lift off the "lids" from the bases. Pull off and discard the soft dough on the undersides of the lids, retaining the crisp brown tops and the indented bottoms. Set aside.

To make the sauce, soften the shallot in half of the Madeira in a medium pan over a low heat until the liquid has reduced, before adding the fish stock and reducing again, to a third of its original volume. Add the cream, simmer for 2 minutes, then add the remaining Madeira. Season well with salt and pepper. Push the sauce through a fine sieve and keep warm.

To finish the dish, pat the scallops with kitchen paper to make sure that they are dry, then slice them in half horizontally. Turn them in the olive oil with a pinch of salt. Quickly sear the scallops on both sides in a very hot, dry frying pan. Pop the pastry cases in the oven for 1 minute if you need to reheat them.

Assemble the finished pastry boxes by putting a spoonful of mushroom fricassée in the bottom of each one and filling it with scallops and some of the sauce. Sprinkle with the

chives and tarragon, and put the lid on top. Scatter the tomatoes around the outside of the little pastry box and serve immediately.

TIP: *To prepare and open scallops, scrub them thoroughly first. Holding the scallop firmly in your non-working hand, flat shell uppermost, insert a long thin and flexible knife between the top and bottom shells. Keep the blade as close as possible to the inside of the top flat shell (to avoid damaging the scallop meat inside). Slide the knife from side to side to sever the muscle holding the two shells together.*

Open up the two shells. The scallop will be sitting in the rounded bottom shell. Detach the scallop, using your knife, again being careful not to cut into the meat. Remove and discard the viscera and frilly membrane, and keep only the white scallop meat and the orange coral. Rinse very lightly before use.

Paella

Although I start this Spanish paella off with chicken, it is really a showcase for fish, including here squid, monkfish, prawns and mussels. You can leave the chicken out if you like, but the flavour will be less intense. You will need a large pan, preferably a paella pan, otherwise a large sauté pan or frying pan.

Serves 8

1 small chicken
olive oil
1 tsp paprika
½ large Spanish onion, sliced
500g (1lb 2oz) ripe tomatoes, skinned (p.146), seeded and chopped
1 red sweet pepper, seeded and chopped
2 garlic cloves, chopped
2 bay leaves
1 tbsp chopped marjoram
at least 400ml (14fl oz) Chicken Stock (p.206)
good pinch of saffron threads
100g (3½oz) chorizo, sliced
1 large squid

450g (1lb) monkfish, cut into chunks
6 raw tiger prawns
200ml (7fl oz) white wine
500g (1lb 2oz) mussels, cleaned and bearded (p.17)
200g (5½oz) risotto rice
50g (1¾) French beans, cooked and refreshed

Garnish
handful of stoned black olives
2 tbsp chopped parsley
1 lemon, cut into wedges

First cut the chicken into ten small pieces. Add about 3 tbsp olive oil to a large pan and fry the chicken pieces on all sides until brown. Add the paprika and onion, and soften the onion for about 5 minutes on a low heat. Now add the tomatoes, red pepper, garlic, bay leaves, marjoram, chicken stock and saffron and cook for 20 minutes on a low heat. In another pan dry-fry the chorizo until brown on all sides, then remove.

Clean the squid by removing the contents of the body and wash thoroughly. Cut off the tentacles and cut the body into rings. Brown the squid and its tentacles in the chorizo pan with 1 tbsp of olive oil, followed by the monkfish and tiger prawns. This will give some richness. Remove from the pan and leave to one side.

In a large saucepan boil the wine, add the mussels and steam for 2 minutes until they just open. Reserve the wine and mussel liquid and put the mussels to one side. Remove half of them from their shells. Now add the rice and the strained mussel liquid to the chicken and tomatoes, and continue cooking on a low heat for 15 minutes. Add the fish, chorizo, French beans and shelled mussels. Cover and cook for a further 15 minutes or until the rice is just tender.

Garnish with the olives, shell-on mussels, chopped parsley and lemon wedges. Serve from the pan and let the guests help themselves.

Red Mullet with Saffron, Roasted Red Pepper Risotto and Parmesan Crisps

This must be one of my most colourful dishes: you have the red skin of the mullet, its white flesh, the red-flecked risotto, the yellow and cream crisps, the black olives (they're a good addition) and the fresh green of the basil. What's more, the whole thing tastes as good as it looks – a feast for the senses.

Serves 4

4 whole red mullet, about 175g (6oz) each,
    scaled, cleaned and filleted
plain flour for dredging
salt and pepper
2 tbsp olive oil

Saffron cream
good pinch of saffron threads
4 tbsp crème fraîche

To serve
1 recipe Roasted Red Pepper Risotto (p.23)
4 Parmesan crisps (p.23)
8 basil leaves
8 black olives, stoned and finely diced
    (optional)

Use 1 tsp of the risotto fish stock to soak the saffron threads for 20 minutes. Meanwhile, make the risotto and Parmesan crisps.

While the risotto is cooking, stir the saffron and fish stock infusion through the crème fraîche until well combined. Cover and refrigerate until needed.

Season the red mullet fillets well on both sides with salt and pepper, and dust with flour. Heat the oil in a large heavy frying pan over a medium heat. Add the fish fillets, skin-side down, and fry for 2–3 minutes on each side.

To serve, put a spoonful of risotto in the centre of each plate. Arrange two red mullet fillets on top of each pile of risotto. Garnish with a spoonful of the saffron cream. Top with the basil, and scatter over the black olives (if using). Garnish each serving with a Parmesan crisp and serve immediately.

Roast Cod with Cannellini Beans and Pancetta

This is one of those simple dishes that everyone loves, because it is easy, effective and very tasty. All you need are good quality ingredients and a certain amount of care in the cooking. With the beans and cod, the only other thing you might want is a well-dressed green salad.

Serves 4

4 cod (or haddock) fillets, about
   180g (6¼oz) each
2 tbsp olive oil
sea salt, salt and pepper
deep-fried sage (p.29)
braised cannellini beans
250g (9oz) dried cannellini beans
1 small onion, finely chopped

2 tbsp olive oil
100g piece pancetta, cut into batons
1 garlic clove, finely chopped
500ml Chicken Stock (p.206)
4 tomatoes, skinned (p.146) and seeded
1 tbsp chopped oregano
2 tbsp chopped parsley

Preheat the oven to 220°C (425°F/Gas 7). First drain the beans, then put them in a pan and cover with fresh water by at least 10cm. Bring to the boil and boil steadily for 10 minutes. Skim, then lower the heat, cover and simmer for 1½ hours. Drain well.

In a large saucepan soften the onion in the olive oil for 3 minutes over a low heat, then add the pancetta and garlic and cook for a couple of minutes longer. Now add the drained beans and stock, and simmer for 20 minutes. Finally, add the tomatoes and continue to cook for about 10 minutes longer. Season with salt and pepper and, just before serving, add the chopped oregano and parsley.

Fry the cod, skin-side down, in a little oil for a minute or so. Sprinkle with a little sea salt. Transfer the fish to a baking dish, place in the preheated oven and cook for 5 minutes.

Serve the cod skin-side up on the warm beans and garnish with crispy sage.

Swinton Trout Lasagne with Basil Pesto

I love lasagne, a combination of delicious home-made pasta, a protein or vegetable ingredient and a smooth sauce. Here, I've served a fishy lasagne with a basil pesto, which is unusual but very tasty – and it looks good, too!

Serves 4–6

1 quantity pasta for lasagne (p.215)
30g (1oz) butter
3 shallots, finely diced
4 medium trout (salmon can be used
   instead), skinned and filleted
2 tbsp very finely chopped dill
salt and pepper
30g (1oz) Parmesan cheese, freshly grated

Béchamel sauce
50g (1¾oz) butter
50g (1¾oz) plain flour
450ml (15fl oz) milk
pinch of freshly grated nutmeg

To serve
1 quantity Basil Pesto (p.218)

First, make and roll the pasta as described on p.215 until you have long lasagne-shaped ribbons. Half-cook the pasta in boiling salted water for 1 minute. Drain and lay on a damp tea towel without overlapping the strips. Cover with cling film or another damp cloth until ready to use. (I use damp cloth on damp cloth, with loads of layers.)

Preheat the oven to 180°C (350°F/Gas 4). Melt the butter in a medium pan over a low heat and soften the shallots for 1 minute. Keep to one side.

Make the béchamel sauce. Melt the butter in a pan over a low heat, add the flour and, using a wooden spoon, stir constantly for 1 minute. Add the milk gradually, stirring all the time, and cook slowly until thick. Season with salt, pepper and a pinch of nutmeg. Now add the softened shallots and stir through. Allow to cool.

Cut the trout fillets in half horizontally so that you have 16 thin slices. Butter an ovenproof dish of about 24 x 20cm (9½ x 8in) and put a tiny bit of béchamel sauce on the bottom, with some of the strips of pasta. Next, put some trout on top, followed by some dill, sauce, then pasta, dill, trout and sauce, building up layers and seasoning with salt and pepper as you go. Finish with a layer of pasta and the last of the béchamel sauce on top. Sprinkle over the Parmesan.

Bake in the oven for 30–40 minutes. Serve cut into slices with the pesto.

Individual Fish Pies with Baby Leeks and Lemon-glazed Carrots

Fish pie to me is such comfort food; it's very special. It's wonderful for a dinner party, but it makes a really good lunch dish, too. And it's always a treat, especially when someone else makes it! This is quite a luxurious version, with sole, plaice, prawns and mussels, and it's very tasty.

Serves 4

100g (3½oz) unsalted butter
600g (1lb 5oz) filleted fish off the bone
   (lemon sole, plaice, haddock, including
   some prawns)
325ml (11fl oz) full-fat milk
75ml (2½fl oz) dry white wine
1 shallot, peeled and roughly chopped
250g (9oz) mussels, cleaned and
   bearded (p.17)
50g (1¾oz) plain flour
salt and pepper
½ fennel bulb, finely sliced
handful of tarragon leaves

Topping
600g (1lb 5oz) floury potatoes (such as

Maris Piper), peeled and quartered
75g (2½oz) unsalted butter
100ml (3½fl oz) full-fat milk
2 tsp finely and freshly grated
   Parmesan cheese

Lemon-glazed Carrots
30 baby carrots, trimmed and scrubbed
2 tsp caster sugar
50g (1¾oz) unsalted butter
finely grated zest and juice of ½ lemon
1 tbsp finely chopped flat-leaf parsley

To serve
1 quantity Baby Leeks with Tomato and
   Herb Vinaigrette (p.131)

Preheat the oven to 200°C (400°F/Gas 6). Lightly grease four small pie dishes about 12 x 7.5cm (5 x 3in) with butter.

Put the fish fillets in a large ovenproof dish and pour the milk over. Bake in the oven for 10–15 minutes until the fish is just cooked. Remove the fish, reserving the milk for the white sauce, and leave until cool enough to handle. Once cooled, carefully remove the skin and any bones from the fish, and flake the flesh into chunks.

Bring the wine and shallot to the boil in a large pan, and add the cleaned mussels. Cover and steam for 5 minutes until all the shells have opened. As usual, discard any that remain closed. Using a fine sieve, drain the mussels over a large jug, reserving the liquid. Remove the mussel meat from the shells.

In a small saucepan, melt half the butter over a low heat and add the flour. Cook for 1 minute, being careful not to brown. Now slowly add the milk that the fish was cooked in, stirring all the time, and cook until it thickens. Season well with salt and pepper.

Soften the fennel in the remaining butter, then transfer to the buttered pie dishes. Arrange the flaked fish, mussels and prawns on top, then sprinkle with the tarragon leaves. Pour the white sauce over the seafood and fennel, turning the ingredients as you pour so that everything is evenly coated. Leave to cool.

To make the topping, bring a pan of salted water to the boil and cook the potatoes for 15 minutes until tender. Drain well, then pass through a fine sieve. Warm the butter and milk together in a small pan and add to the potatoes, mashing until smooth. Mix in the Parmesan and season to taste with salt and pepper. Put the potatoes in a piping bag and pipe the mash over the top of the fish. Set aside until ready to bake.

Meanwhile, make the lemon-glazed carrots. Put the carrots in a pan, add the sugar and butter and enough water to barely cover, and bring to the boil. Reduce the heat and simmer for about 2 minutes until the carrots just give when pressed with the point of a sharp knife. Remove the carrots from the liquid and keep to one side. Now add the lemon zest and juice to the carrot liquid and reduce until thick. Roll the carrots in the resulting juices until just glazed. Season to taste with salt and pepper, and keep warm until ready to serve.

Bake the fish pies in the oven for 20–30 minutes until the potato is golden and the pie warmed through. Warm through the baby leeks and the carrots if needed.

To serve, place each fish pie on a large serving plate. Arrange the leeks to one side, and spoon over some of the tomato and herb vinaigrette. Serve with the carrots.

Confit of Salmon with Courgette Spaghetti

This is such a simple way of cooking salmon. It's particularly good served with the deep-fried shallots, but you can leave those out if you like. The dish needs the courgettes, though, cooked minimally as "spaghetti", and they look and taste great. The courgette spaghetti is such a nice salad idea, and it is good, too, with fishcakes, served either as a starter or main course.

Serves 4

olive oil, enough to cover
4 salmon fillets, skin on, 180g (6oz) each
3 star anise
8 black peppercorns
salt and pepper

Courgette spaghetti
4 courgettes, trimmed
1 red chilli, deseeded and chopped
1 garlic clove, finely chopped
1 tbsp olive oil
1 tbsp finely snipped chives

Deep-fried shallots (optional)
4 shallots
1 tbsp plain flour for dredging

Eastern vinaigrette
150ml (5fl oz) extra virgin olive oil
juice of 1 lemon
2 tbsp light soy sauce
2 tsp saké
2 tsp mirin
1 tsp caster sugar

In a heavy saucepan large enough to take the four fillets, heat enough olive oil to immerse the salmon with the spices to 60°C (140°F).

Make sure that all the bones have been removed from the salmon, then put the fillets in the oil skin-side down. Do *not* allow the temperature to rise. When you see the white protein bubbles appearing, the fish is done. This takes about 20 minutes.

While the fish is cooking, cut the courgettes, either using a mandoline or by hand, very thinly like spaghetti. Gently soften the chilli and garlic in a little olive oil over a low heat. Remove from the heat and add the courgettes. Mix very carefully, then drain. Season with salt and pepper and sprinkle with the chives.

Using a fish slice or wide spatula, remove the fish from the oil and keep warm. Remove and discard the spices. Increase the heat, and now add the shallots (if using), dredged in flour and any excess shaken off; deep-fry for 30–60 seconds until golden and crisp.

Make up the vinaigrette by whisking all the ingredients together.

To serve, put a small pile of courgettes in the middle of each plate, top with a piece of salmon, then surround with the dressing. Finish with the crispy shallots (if using).

Poultry

Chicken is a good protein source, offering a variety of flavours and textures – such as the different white breast and darker leg meat – and it goes a very long way. It's one of the most versatile meats you can buy.

As with fish, I would always advise that you buy the product whole. If you buy a whole chicken and cut it up yourself, taking the breasts and legs off, you are also getting the carcass, which you can use to make a wonderful stock for soups and sauces. But you must buy chicken wisely. I like to use organic, free-range and corn-fed poultry, but I do realise that these can be expensive. You can find poultry that will have been reared in a humane way, and this will only be a little dearer than battery. But please make sure to avoid like the plague any packs of chicken thighs or drumsticks at rock-bottom prices; just stop to think about how these will have been produced.

You can buy organic poussins as well. I love the flavour of guinea fowl, but because the flesh can be so dry it is less versatile than chicken. There are several varieties of domestic duck, Barbary and Gressingham among them, and what you look for here is a lovely dry, plump, fresh-looking skin.

The poultry recipes here, like those in the fish chapter, are for special occasions, and involve many elements, but as usual you can do much of the preparation well in advance.

As some of the recipes involve slightly more difficult preparation techniques, I will outline a couple of them here (see also the photographs on p.79).

To cut a bird into four pieces, remove the two whole legs (thigh and drumstick) using a sharp knife or poultry shears. Cut the top two joints off the wings (use these for stock), leaving the wings still attached to the breasts. You are left with the crown (the two breasts on the bone, plus wings) and the backbone, which you remove completely (and again save for stock). Then cut the breast into two pieces along the breastbone.

To cut these pieces further, into eight to ten pieces (for the fricassée perhaps), cut the legs into two, thigh and drumstick, and then cut the wings off, with a little of the breast. Depending on the size of the bird, you can leave the remaining breast as it is, or cut it into two pieces. Now you should have four leg pieces, two wing pieces and two to four breast pieces.

To bone a poultry leg, lay it on the work surface, exposed knuckle-side upwards. With a small sharp knife, cut along the length of the thigh bone and then work in and around the bone with the knife point, to release the flesh from the bone down to the knuckle. Pull this out. Now perform the same operation from the knuckle down to the end of the drumstick. Pull this out carefully as well. You will be left with a nice rectangle of chicken or duck flesh, ready to stuff.

Chicken Stuffed with Chicken Livers, with a Cassis Sauce, Baby Turnips and Parisienne Potatoes

Chicken thighs and legs are by far the tastiest and juiciest parts of the bird. Chicken breasts are lovely, and are what most people might choose, but they are less succulent, and are so easily overcooked. You can get your butcher to bone the legs.

Serves 4

4 whole chicken legs, boned
salt and pepper
12 chicken livers, sinews removed
15g (½oz) butter
2 tsp each of thyme and sage leaves
  (halve this if using dried herbs)
1 garlic clove, finely chopped
16 large spinach leaves
extra virgin olive oil

Cassis sauce
1 leek, chopped
1 carrot, chopped

1 onion, chopped
60g (2oz) cold butter
1 large tbsp redcurrant jelly
200ml (7fl oz) red wine
400ml (14fl oz) Chicken Stock (p.206)
50g (1¾oz) white roux (optional,
  see opposite)
150ml (5fl oz) double cream
a glug of Cassis

To serve
1 quantity Buttered Baby Turnips (p.132)
1 quantity Parisienne Potatoes (p.125)

Preheat the oven to 200°C (400°F/Gas 6). Spread the chicken legs flat on your board, with the skin underneath, and season them with salt and pepper to taste. Dry the livers thoroughly with kitchen paper. Melt the butter in a pan and sear the livers on both sides quickly – do not cook through. Toss them in the thyme, sage and garlic while still warm.

Blanch the spinach for a few seconds in boiling water. Drain well and keep the leaves separate. Put four leaves together, place three chicken livers on top and wrap the livers in the spinach, making a sausage shape. Repeat with the remaining leaves and livers, and place each inside a chicken leg. Bring the sides in slightly and gently bring the skin up to make four parcels. Secure using several pieces of string crossways and one lengthways. Brush the little bundles with olive oil and roast them, uncovered, for 20 minutes in the preheated oven. Remove, and if you think they are not quite cooked then roast for another 5 minutes. Allow them to rest for 5 minutes.

Meanwhile, make the sauce. Cook the leek, carrot and onion in half the butter for 10 minutes, or until soft. Add the redcurrant jelly and wine, and boil to reduce to a syrup. Add the stock and boil to reduce to half. If needed, add a little white roux to thicken. Pass the sauce through a fine sieve, then add the cream and Cassis. Season really well with salt and pepper, then whisk in the remaining butter to make the sauce glossy.

Cut each stuffed chicken leg into three slices. Serve with the sauce and the vegetables.

Fricassée of Chicken with Vermouth and Mushrooms with Herb Pilaff

A simple fricassée, which is full of flavour. It is delicious served with the herb pilaff – the rice and green herbs look and taste good with the chicken – but you could serve plain boiled old or new potatoes, or fettucine instead.

Serves 4

1 chicken
30g (1oz) butter
1 tbsp vegetable oil
250ml (8fl oz) dry vermouth
750ml (1¼ pints) Chicken Stock (p.206)
1 bouquet garni
14 small shallots, peeled and left whole
100g (3½oz) button mushrooms

200ml (7fl oz) double cream
35g (1¼oz) white roux (see tip below)
salt and pepper
8 spring onions, trimmed and finely sliced
1 tbsp finely chopped parsley

To serve
1 quantity Herb Pilaff (p.148)

First joint the chicken into 10 pieces. Put the butter and oil into a large saucepan and lightly brown the chicken pieces on all sides. Deglaze with half the dry vermouth. Now add the chicken stock and bouquet garni and cook without a lid over a low heat for about 20 minutes. Turn the chicken halfway through the cooking time.

Meanwhile cook the shallots in a little of the stock to cover until they are just soft, about 10 minutes. Remove the shallots with a slotted spoon and reserve. Then add the mushrooms to the stock and cook for 5 minutes. Remove the mushrooms using a slotted spoon and add to the shallots.

Remove the chicken and bouquet garni from the stock, and keep the chicken to one side. Turn the heat a little higher, and now add the cream and the white roux to the stock. Bring up to a simmer and continue simmering for 5 minutes. Season well with salt and pepper. Put in the shallots, mushrooms and chicken, and continue cooking for another 5 minutes.

Garnish with the spring onions and chopped parsley. Serve with the pilaff.

TIP:

Beurre manié is equal quantities of butter and flour, blended together (like a roux but not cooked). This will prevent the flour from going lumpy when added to the sauce. Use a little at a time until the desired consistency has been achieved. A white roux takes the idea a little further, cooking the butter and flour together minimally before adding to a liquid. A brown roux thickens as well as adding colour (p.99).

Breast of Corn-fed Chicken with Red Pepper Mousse and Pearl Barley Risotto

Corn-fed chickens, cooked well, are yummy. Here the breasts are wrapped around a mousse and steamed so that they are still moist. (You could do the same with pheasant or guinea fowl as well.) It's a very pretty dish, and you could make it even more colourful by adding some boiled green beans tossed with olive oil and garlic.

Serves 4

4 corn-fed chicken breasts, skinned

Red pepper mousse
1½ red peppers, skinned (p.23) and seeded
150g (5½oz) corn-fed chicken
  breast, skinned
½ small egg white
150ml (5fl oz) double cream
1 tbsp finely chopped parsley
50g (1¾oz) butter

Sauce
1 chicken carcass or a few raw
  chicken bones
1 onion, chopped
1 celery stick, chopped
1 small carrot, chopped
2–3 garlic cloves, chopped

handful of herbs, roughly chopped
200ml (7fl oz) white grape juice
300ml (10fl oz) good strong Chicken
  Stock (p.206)
50g (1¾oz) unsalted butter
1 tbsp plain flour
200ml (7fl oz) double cream
100ml (3½fl oz) dry Madeira wine

Honeyed parsnips
3 tbsp olive oil
3 tbsp sunflower oil
500g (1lb 2oz) parsnips, peeled and
  quartered lengthways
1 rounded tbsp runny honey

To serve
1 quantity Pearl Barley Risotto (p.149)

Start with the mousse. Dice the skinned red peppers very finely. Cook in 20g (¾oz) of the butter until very soft. Strain really well to get all the liquid out. Process the raw chicken breast with the egg white using a food processor or blender. Then add the double cream very carefully. You will be in trouble if you over-process this cream, so use the pulse button to ensure it doesn't curdle. Put the mixture into a bowl and fold in the parsley and cooked red pepper.

Put the chicken breasts between sheets of cling film and bash each into a rectangle. Take a clean sheet of cling film and place on it the bashed chicken breasts. Put a quarter of the red pepper mousse on top of each piece of chicken, on the side nearest to you, then roll them up lightly, like a sushi, into a sausage shape. Using two thumbs, roll and hold it, then roll again to tighten. Make four sausages in this way. Put them into the refrigerator to chill.

To make the sauce, fry the chicken carcass in a large, heavy saucepan until brown on all sides. Then add the onion, celery, carrot, garlic and herbs, and brown them too. Now add the grape juice and stock, and simmer until reduced to half, about 10 minutes.

Strain the vegetables and chicken carcass pieces out of the liquid and discard them. Mix the butter and flour to a *beurre manié* (p.73) and stir a little into the stock mix in a clean saucepan. Bring to the boil again, stirring continuously, then add the double cream and the Madeira. Bring it back to the boil, then let it cool and leave it aside until the last minute.

About 50 minutes before you want to serve, make the honeyed parsnips. Preheat the oven to 200°C (400°F/Gas 6). Pour the oils into a roasting tin and heat in the oven. Meanwhile, bring a pan of salted water to the boil. Cook the parsnip wedges in the boiling water for 3 minutes and drain well. Carefully add them to the hot oil, turning to coat. Put them in the oven for about 20 minutes. Drizzle the honey over and turn them again to evenly coat, then roast for another 20 minutes, until the parsnips are sticky, golden and tender.

Steam-cook the chilled chicken breasts on low for about 20 minutes, turning them over halfway through. Cut off the ends to neaten them, then cut in half at an angle. Place on top of the pearl barley risotto and pour a little of the sauce around. Serve with the honeyed parsnips.

Steamed Chicken Stuffed with Mushroom Mousse, with Lentils and Pink Peppercorns and Parsnips

This is rather a convenient dish, in that it can be mostly prepared in advance; all you have to do at the last minute is the steaming. You can leave the individual elements in the refrigerator, but do remember that if you cook something straight from the refrigerator it is cold, which might mean a couple more minutes of cooking. I've used my favourite porcini, or ceps, again, which can be enjoyed at all times of the year because they dry so well.

Serves 4

4 chicken breasts

Mushroom mousse
15g (½oz) dried porcini mushrooms
1 shallot, finely chopped
50g (1¾oz) butter
150g (5½oz) chicken breast meat
½ egg white
150ml (5fl oz) double cream

salt and pepper
2 tbsp finely chopped parsley

To serve
1 quantity Lentils and Pink Peppercorns (p.145)
1 quantity crispy parsnips (see Crispy Vegetables, p.127)

To start the mushroom mousse, soak the porcini mushrooms in a bowl of cold water for 30 minutes.

Meanwhile take a frying pan and gently soften the shallot in butter over a low heat. Drain the porcini mushrooms (saving the water for stock or sauces), cut them up finely, then add to the shallots and cook for a couple of minutes. Drain and cool.

Process the chicken breast with the egg white using a food processor. Pulse in the cream, taking care not to over-process it as it will curdle. Transfer to a bowl, then fold in the porcini mushroom mixture, season well with salt and pepper, and add the parsley.

Make a horizontal slit into the side of each chicken breast, through the middle but not all the way through, so that the two pieces are still attached. Pipe the mousse mixture into each chicken breast. Wrap in cling film and chill until ready to steam.

Steam the stuffed chicken breasts for 20 minutes, then remove the cling film. Slice the ends off then slice through the middle so that it stands up. To serve, put a spoonful of lentils in the middle of the plate and top with the sliced stuffed chicken breast. Garnish with the crispy fried parsnips. If you like, you can add some green beans and asparagus as well for colour and texture.

Roast Poussin Stuffed with Pilaff, with Chilli Stir-Fry and Piquant Tomato Sauce

Poussins are such perfect birds to do for dinner parties, and, although you might not think so, boning them is good fun. You can prepare the majority of this dish the day before, only needing to roast and stir-fry at the last minute.

Serves 6

3 poussins
½ quantity Herb Pilaff (p.148)
50g (1¾oz) butter, melted

Chilli stir-fry
2 tbsp olive oil
1 garlic clove, finely chopped
2cm (½ x ¾in) piece fresh root ginger, finely chopped
2 red chillies, seeded and finely chopped
1 tsp five-spice powder

6 small pak choi, quartered
18 mangetout, finely sliced
200g (7oz) beansprouts
1½ red peppers, seeded and finely sliced
salt

To serve
1 quantity Potato Fritters (p.122)
1 quantity Piquant Tomato Sauce (p.219)
6 sprigs chervil

Preheat the oven to 190°C (375°F/Gas 5). To bone the poussins, turn each upside down and make an incision along the length of the bone. Cut through the wing and side joint, then cut around the bony central part until you get to the bottom of the carcass, the breast part. Repeat on the other side. Carefully cut the bottom of the carcass away so that you are left with a whole, flat bird, with legs and wings attached. Bone the legs too.

Spread the birds skin-down onto the board. Lift the breasts up, spoon the pilaff onto the skin and fold the breasts back over the pilaff. Pull the skin around the sides and secure each by weaving a skewer through. Turn the birds on their sides and tie the legs together with string, so they look like miniscule turkeys. This can be done well in advance.

Brush the poussins with butter and roast in the preheated oven for 35 minutes, then take them out. Baste again and return to the oven for 10 minutes. Keep them warm while you finish the stir-fry, the potato fritters and tomato sauce.

Meanwhile, start the stir-fry. Heat the oil in a large frying pan or wok and add the garlic, ginger, chilli, five-spice powder, then the vegetables. Make sure the heat is turned right up. Stir continuously for 5 minutes, then add some salt.

Carefully cut the poussins in half. To serve put a small pile of stir-fry in the middle of the plate and top with half a poussin. Put three potato fritters on the side and add a little tomato sauce. Garnish with chervil.

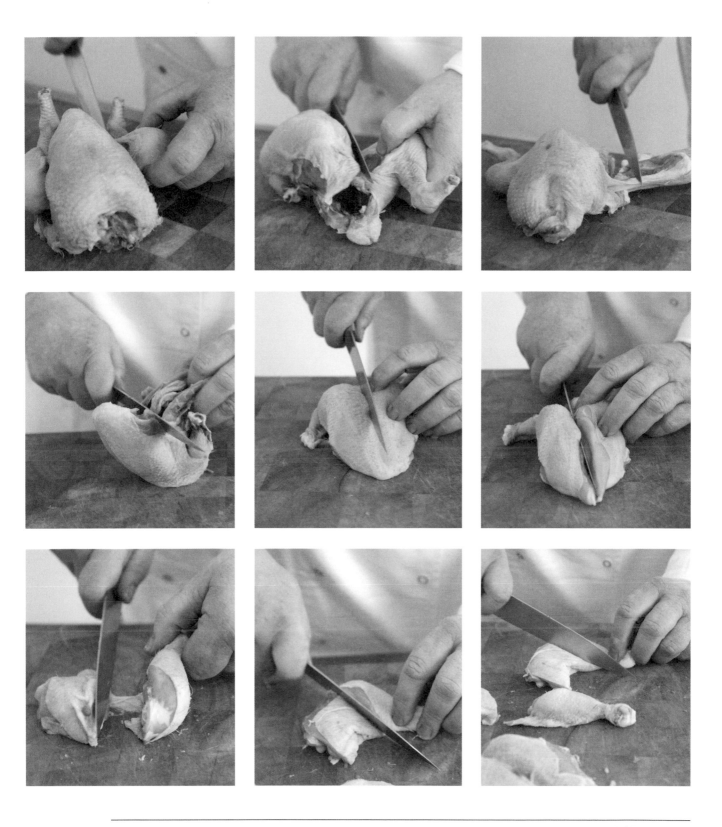

Poussin Stuffed with Pork, Chestnut and Mushroom Farce, with a Marsala Sauce

This is a recipe with an Italian influence. I think of it as almost a store cupboard dish, as you can use those very good vacuum-packed chestnuts and the lovely dried porcini. It's a wintery type of dish, although the beetroots are more spring. The farce would make a very good stuffing for a Christmas turkey too!

Serves 4

15g (½oz) dried porcini mushrooms
2 poussins
15g (½oz) butter
60g (2oz) flat mushrooms, coarsely chopped
120g (4¼oz) peeled and cooked chestnuts, finely chopped
200g (7oz) pork shoulder, minced
salt and pepper
goose fat

Sauce
20g (¾oz) unsalted butter
1 garlic clove, finely chopped

100g (3½oz) flat mushrooms, finely chopped
100ml (3½fl oz) Marsala wine
100ml (3½fl oz) double cream
150ml (5fl oz) Chicken Stock (p.206), reduced to 100ml (3½fl oz)

To serve
1 quantity Roast Baby Beetroots (p.132)
1 quantity Asparagus and Beans (p.142)
1 quantity crispy beetroots (optional, see Crispy Vegetables, p.127)
4 sprigs chervil

Soak the porcini for 30 minutes in enough warm water to cover. Meanwhile, bone the poussins, leaving the leg bones and the wings (p.78).

Preheat the oven to 190°C (375°F/Gas 5). Drain the porcini really well, squeezing out any excess liquid (and keeping all the liquid for stock), and finely chop.

Sauté the porcini in the butter with the flat mushrooms and chestnuts until soft, about 5 minutes. Leave to cool completely before mixing with the minced pork. Season well with salt and pepper.

Stuff the poussins with the pork farce, then either sew up the backs of the birds, or secure with a wooden skewer. Smear the poussins with goose fat and roast in the oven for 35 minutes.

To make the sauce, melt the butter in a small pan, then add the garlic and mushrooms and cook gently for 3 minutes. Add the Marsala and boil for another minute to evaporate the alcohol. Add the cream and stock and reduce by about half, then liquidise. Pass through a fine sieve over a pan. Return to the heat and adjust the consistency by either reducing further if it is too thin or adding more stock if it is too thick. Season well with salt and pepper.

Remove the skewers from the poussins and cut the birds in half, and then in half again. Be careful, as the birds will be pretty solid with the pork farce. To serve, put the roasted beetroot in the middle of each plate and top with two pieces of poussin. Garnish with beans and asparagus, and surround with the lovely Marsala and mushroom sauce. Put a few crispy beetroots on top, if using, and finally garnish with a sprig of chervil.

TIP: *When securing stuffed whole birds or stuffed portions of birds or meat, I quite often use those thin, wooden Japanese stick-type skewers; you buy them in bunches, and I find them very useful indeed.*

Poussins with Cherries, Polenta Cakes and Roasted Shallots

I love recipes like this because I am keen on wrapping things in pieces of bacon – there's so much flavour. This is not unlike a coq au vin, but I have married the bird and bacon with cherries, which is a great combination. You could, of course, use a small chicken here instead of the poussins, and cut it into smaller pieces.

Serves 4

3 poussins, boned (p.78) and quartered
12 slices very thin streaky bacon
2 tbsp olive oil
2 tsp plain flour
300ml (10fl oz) double cream
salt and pepper

Marinade
1 celery stick
1 small leek
1 carrot
1 onion

2 garlic cloves
1 bottle red wine

Cherry compôte
100ml (3½fl oz) red wine
100ml (3½fl oz) port
250g (9oz) black cherries, stoned

To serve
1 quantity Polenta Cake (p.149)
1 quantity Roasted Shallots (p.128)

To prepare the marinade, chop all the vegetables and mix with the wine in a large bowl. Wrap each piece of poussin in a slice of bacon and secure with a cocktail stick. Put into the marinade for several hours. (If you haven't time, you can miss out this marination.)

Preheat the oven to 200°C (400°F/Gas 6). Take out the poussin pieces and pat dry. Strain the marinade into a jug. Keep both liquid and vegetables.

Heat the oil in a heavy casserole and brown the poussin pieces on all sides. Remove and set aside. Put the vegetables from the marinade into the casserole, turn them, sprinkle over the flour and add the marinade liquid. Bring to boiling point and return the poussin. Cover with a lid and cook in the oven for about 25 minutes.

To make the cherry compôte, bring the wine and port to the boil and reduce by half. Add the cherries, return to the boil and simmer for 2–3 minutes. Strain, reserving the liquid and putting the cherries to one side.

Transfer the poussin to a serving dish (removing the cocktail sticks). Keep warm. Put the sauce through a fine sieve and return to a clean pan. Over a low heat reduce it by half. Add the cream and the liquid from the cherries, and stir for 15 minutes. Season well, then add the poussin and the cherries. Serve with the polenta cakes and shallots.

Fettucine with Duck Sauce

Known in Italy as *fettuccine al sugo d'anatra*, this is a delicious combination of tender home-made ribbons of pasta and an intense duck sauce. It is ideal for a casual lunch dish, or you could serve it Italian style as a first course, when it would serve about six people. Duck breasts are delicious, but duck legs are so much juicier (as are chicken legs).

Serves 4

350g (12oz) fettucine
2 tbsp chopped parsley

Duck sauce
4 large duck legs
2 shallots, diced
60g (2oz) celery, diced
70g (2¼oz) carrot, diced
1 leek, thinly sliced
50ml (1¾fl oz) olive oil

30g (1oz) butter
leaves from 1 sprig thyme
1 tbsp tomato purée
2 tbsp brandy
100ml (3½fl oz) dry Marsala wine
200ml (7fl oz) Chicken Stock (p.206)
finely grated rind and juice of 1 small
  orange
50g (1¾oz) large green olives, stoned
salt and pepper

To make the sauce, remove all the meat from the duck legs and dice it finely along with most of the fat. Soften the shallots, celery, carrot and leek in the oil and butter in a pan over a medium heat for 5–6 minutes, add the diced duck meat and fat and then brown it all over. Add the thyme leaves, the tomato purée diluted in the brandy, the Marsala and the chicken stock. Cover and cook over a low heat for a good hour until tender.

Add the orange rind and juice, and boil to reduce a little. (Do use a small orange or the rind and juice can turn the sauce too bitter.) Cut the olives into thin strips and add to heat through.

Meanwhile, cook the fettucine in boiling salted water until *al dente*, about 2 minutes if using fresh fettucine, or longer if shop-bought.

Taste the sauce for seasoning, and then toss with the drained fettuccine and a little chopped parsley.

Roast Duck Breasts with Onion Tart and Butternut Squash Gratin

You've got a wonderful combination of flavours here. Duck is delicious and goes so well with butternut squash. The little onion tart is a great garnish, and it is really delicious to eat, particularly if made with home-made puff pastry. You will need some little individual tart tins.

Serves 4

4 Gressingham duck breasts
2 tbsp walnut oil
salt and pepper

Butternut squash gratin
1 large butternut squash
90g (3oz) butter, melted
1 tsp chopped rosemary

Sauce
1 shallot, finely chopped
20g (¾oz) butter
2 tbsp honey

100ml (3½fl oz) red wine
50ml (1¾fl oz) soy sauce
250ml (8fl oz) stock (duck or chicken, p.206)
60g (2oz) butter
3 tbsp brandy

To serve
1 quantity Onion Tarte Tatin (p.130)
1 leek, cut into very fine julienne strips
sunflower oil, for deep-frying

Carefully score the skin of the duck breasts. Marinate the duck pieces in the walnut oil, ideally for a couple of hours.

Preheat the oven to 150°C (300°F/Gas 2). Start making the butternut squash gratin (this is actually better done in advance). Peel the squash and, using a mandolin, slice it very finely (see p.88). Then layer it in a well-buttered gratin dish about 20cm (8in) square, sprinkling it with rosemary and salt and brushing melted butter between the layers, finishing with melted butter. Bake in the oven for 1 hour. Remove and press it down to seal it, perhaps with a weight on top (this will make it quite thin). Allow it to cool, and then cut into 4 x 7cm (1½ x 2¾in) circles with a round cutter. Place these on a baking dish ready to heat through before serving.

To make the sauce (this can also be done well in advance), take a frying pan and soften the shallot in the butter over a medium heat for a few minutes. Add the honey and let it cook until it becomes slightly caramelised, then add the red wine and soy sauce. Let it bubble up and reduce to a syrupy consistency. Add the stock and let it boil briskly for a further 5 minutes until it becomes a little thick. Strain it, season with salt and pepper to taste, and set it aside.

Increase the temperature of the oven to 220°C (425°F/Gas 7).

Deep-fry the leeks in sunflower oil at 170°C (350°F). Drain very well.

Remove the duck breasts from the walnut oil, dry them and sear them, skin-side down, very quickly, about 2 minutes, until crisp. Roast the duck breasts in the oven for a further 6 minutes, turning halfway through. Leave the duck to rest for 10 minutes. (You could roast it before dinner, and leave it to rest while you are having your first course.) While the duck is resting, you could be baking (at a slightly lower temperature) or heating through the tarte tatin.

Bring the sauce to the boil and whisk in the butter, followed by the brandy. Let it simmer for a moment or two and season it with salt and pepper to taste.

Serve the duck with a round of squash gratin, garnished with some deep-fried leek, alongside an onion tarte tatin. Pour the sauce around.

Guinea Fowl with Peas, Beans and Lentils with Cauliflower Purée

I go to Italy quite a lot, and we cook and eat a lot of guinea fowl out there. It's one of those birds that can be incredibly dry, therefore needs to be cooked wrapped up in some way and in lots of flavours to keep it moist. Here I'm almost steaming it within a package of foil. It's very simple, but you have lots of flavour. You should never overcook guinea fowl.

Serves 4

handful each of sage and thyme leaves
2 sprigs rosemary
8 tbsp chopped pancetta or dry-cured
  streaky bacon
salt and pepper
2 plump guinea fowl
juice of 2 lemons
2 tbsp olive oil

Peas, beans and lentils
50g (1¾oz) Puy lentils
1 garlic clove, left whole
500g (1lb 2oz) peas in their pods
500g (1lb 2oz) broad beans in their pods
50g (1¾oz) butter
2 tbsp chopped mint

To serve
1 quantity Cauliflower Purée (p.134)
20 Deep-Fried Sage Leaves (p.29)

Preheat the oven to 200°C (400°F/Gas 6). Chop the herbs and mix with the pancetta and some salt and pepper. Stuff the guinea fowls with half of this mixture. Take a large sheet of foil, put it in a roasting tin, then lay the two guinea fowl on top. Add the remaining mixture to the base of the tin, and sprinkle the birds with the lemon juice and olive oil. Close the foil tightly around the birds.

Roast in the oven for 45 minutes, then open up the foil and roast for a further 25 minutes to allow the birds to brown.

While the birds are cooking, boil the lentils with the garlic until tender (about 25 minutes), then drain thoroughly. Shell the peas and beans, and cook them separately in boiling water until tender. Drain the peas and beans, then mix them with the lentils. Add the butter and toss to coat. Then add the mint, and season with salt and pepper to taste.

Carve the guinea fowl. Place on a bed of lentils on individual warmed plates, and garnish with crispy sage. Serve with the cauliflower purée.

Meat

I always buy meat carefully, sourcing it from local farmers if possible. This is easier in the country, but meat-eaters in towns and cities can still acquire good free-range or organic meat by buying from reputable butchers and game-dealers.

I have always been very keen on lamb, a love deepened by my years in the Hebrides – the lamb there being so sweet. I think the best lamb should be older rather than younger, and I like it hung for no more than ten days. When buying lamb for special occasions, it is very important that you know where it comes from (preferably not the other side of the world). I also find it interesting to know the breed I'm buying, and quite often have fantastic conversations with my suppliers. Never hesitate to ask questions: the professionals are proud of their work, and are always willing to fill you in on arcane details.

The lamb recipes here are a mixed bunch, revealing quite a lot of influences. There is a slow-cooked dish, using shoulder, which I think is the most flavourful cut. The rack of lamb and best end of lamb recipes are definitely for special occasions, and I think you will be pleased with the garnishes I suggest (but of course you can mix and match from the vast selection in the vegetables and accompaniments chapter).

Beef is another favourite meat. In a restaurant, I would always choose a T-bone steak, which consists of the strip loin on one side and the fillet on the other. I think this has the most flavour of all steaks. I haven't given a steak recipe here, but I think you'll like my miniature steak and kidney puddings with their quite unusual enclosing, suet crust pastry.

Most pork available these days hasn't got enough fat for me – it's been bred out – and the majority of the flavour comes from the fat. I like Gloucester Old Spot pork (and the sausages we get are to die for). Belly of pork, although considered cheap, is a delicious cut and great for a dinner party, as is tenderloin.

I'm very fond of game, both furred and feathered. I haven't included any game bird recipes, but I hope you will excuse me including three venison recipes (and one rabbit). Venison meat is delicious both farmed and wild, and it is low in cholesterol and fat. Always keep an eye open when visiting farm shops and farmers' markets: if they have venison, possibly more than you need for a specific occasion, buy while you have the opportunity and freeze it for later. All meat freezes well.

Meat cookery isn't difficult, once you understand the basics. The one great and indisputable rule is to allow meat to rest after cooking. During that 15 or 20 minutes, under foil to retain as much heat as possible, the blood redistributes itself and the flesh relaxes, which makes for increased tenderness and better eating.

Herb-crusted Rack of Lamb with Spinach Mousse, Pea Pancake and Flageolet Beans

Rack of lamb is one of life's delights, I think – with its sweet, tender flesh, enhanced traditionally by pulses, and here, perhaps not so traditionally, by a spinach mousse and a delicious little pea pancake.

Serves 4

2 tsp thyme leaves
2 tbsp finely chopped parsley
1 tbsp finely chopped chives
1 tbsp black peppercorns, crushed
1 tbsp olive oil
2 garlic cloves, crushed
4 racks of lamb, 3 ribs each, French trimmed (bones well trimmed), fat removed
Dijon mustard

Sauce
1kg (2¼lb) lamb bones, chopped into small pieces
2 tbsp vegetable oil
1 onion, halved

2 garlic cloves, roughly chopped
1 carrot, roughly chopped
1 sprig thyme
2 tomatoes, roughly chopped
½ bottle red wine
1 tbsp redcurrant jelly
3 sprigs rosemary
Chicken Stock (p.206) or water, to cover
25g (scant 1oz) *beurre manié* (p.73)

To serve
1 quantity Braised Flageolets (p.145)
1 quantity Spinach Mousse (p.138)
1 quantity Pea Pancakes (p.135)

Mix together the herbs, peppercorns, olive oil and garlic together on a flat plate. Sear the racks on all sides in the oil, then brush with mustard all over. Coat the racks with the herb mixture. Cover and refrigerate for at least 2 hours.

Next prepare the sauce. Sear the lamb bones and meat trimmings from the rack in the oil in a large saucepan over a very low heat for 25 minutes, until quite brown. Add the onion, garlic, carrot and thyme, and cook for 4–5 minutes until they catch colour as well. Add the tomatoes and cook for 5 minutes. Add the wine, redcurrant jelly and rosemary, and reduce to a syrupy consistency before adding enough chicken stock or water to cover the bones well. Simmer for 45 minutes, skimming as you go, but without stirring.

During this time, you can be preparing the spinach mousse (in an oven preheated to 170°C (325°F/Gas 3) and starting the flageolets.

Pass the finished sauce-stock through a fine sieve into a clean pan and return to the boil. Reduce to simmer until reduced by half. Stir a little *beurre manié* (p.73) at a time through the reduced sauce, allowing it to cook out before adding more, until the desired thickness is achieved. Cover and set aside, reheating on serving.

Turn up the oven to 200°C (400°F/Gas 6). Heat the remaining olive oil in a large ovenproof frying pan over a high heat and sear the racks of lamb, herb-side down, for a couple of minutes to achieve a good colour. Turn them right-side up and transfer to the oven to roast for about 10–12 minutes. Remove, cover with foil and leave to rest while you finish the mousse and flageolet beans, and prepare and cook the pea pancakes.

Now slice each rack of lamb into cutlets. Spoon some of the flageolet beans onto the centre of each serving plate, arranging three or four of the lamb cutlets on top. Spoon a little of the sauce over. Serve the spinach mousse to the side with the pea pancakes.

Best End of Lamb with Cauliflower Purée, Ratatouille and Braised Shallots

I just adore the combination of lamb and cauliflower. For me, these flavours work really well together. I often serve this Barnsley cut of saddle with braised flageolets (p.145) instead of ratatouille. The dish looks good with a few black olives strewn about.

Serves 6

½ lamb saddle (the Barnsley end or fillet end, with loin and fillet together)
salt and pepper
olive oil
1 tbsp each of finely chopped parsley, mint and coriander leaves

Braised shallots
12 shallots
60g (2oz) butter

Sauce
bones from the lamb
1 tbsp olive oil
150ml (5fl oz) red wine
2 garlic cloves, chopped
2 sprigs rosemary
2 rounded tsp redcurrant jelly
250ml (8fl oz) Veal Jus or Meat Stock (p.207)

Garnish
1 quantity Cauliflower Purée (p.134)
1 quantity Ratatouille (p.144)
a few sprigs mint

First season the Barnsley ends with salt and pepper to taste, then brush some olive oil all over. Now roll them in the chopped herbs, then roll in cling film to make a cylindrical shape. Refrigerate for 2 hours.

To cook the shallots, wrap in a large doubled sheet of foil with the butter, and cook in an oven preheated to 200°C (400°F/Gas 6) for about an hour.

Sear the meat on all sides in hot oil in a frying pan, then transfer to the oven and cook for about 6–8 minutes. Remove and allow to rest for another 8 minutes.

To make the sauce, brown the bones on all sides in a little oil in a medium pan. Pour the red wine into the pan with the garlic, rosemary and redcurrant jelly, and reduce to a syrup, or about 1 tbsp. Now add the veal jus or stock and reduce again by half. Strain through a fine sieve and season well with salt and pepper.

To serve, slice the lamb and place on top of a portion of ratatouille on each plate. Then add a quenelle of cauliflower purée and two braised shallots. Garnish with mint, and surround with the sauce.

Tagine of Lamb Wrapped in Aubergine with Preserved Lemons and Couscous Salad

I'm a great lover of Moroccan food, and this dish, with little morsels of tasty food, encapsulates many classic Moroccan ideas and flavours. The preserved lemons you can buy in jars are so good these days. They are really important in this dish – you only use the rind – lifting all the flavours. And you don't really have to wrap the tagine up, you could just serve it as a tasty stew by itself with the couscous.

Serves 6

3 large aubergines
olive oil
salt and pepper

Tagine
1 small shoulder of lamb, boned
4 tbsp olive oil
1 onion, chopped
¾ bottle red wine
4 garlic cloves
3cm (1in) piece fresh root ginger, finely chopped
4 tsp ground cinnamon
good pinch of saffron threads
2 tbsp clear honey

150g (5½oz) raisins
6 tbsp finely chopped coriander
50g (1¾oz) flaked almonds
at least 1 litre (1¾ pints) Chicken Stock (p.206)
2 tsp tomato purée
50g (1¾oz) brown roux (see tip opposite)

To serve
1 quantity Couscous Salad with Lemon (p.146)
12 small vine tomatoes, with stalks
caster sugar
2 preserved lemons, skins only, finely sliced
olive oil

Preheat the oven to 150°C (300°F/Gas 2). To make the lamb tagine, cut the lamb into small cubes. In a large casserole, heat the oil and brown the meat all over for a few minutes, then remove from the dish. Soften the onion in the same pan, adding more oil if necessary, then add the wine and deglaze until reduced to half. Return the lamb to the casserole with all the other ingredients for the tagine, cover and cook in the preheated oven for 2 hours. This is best done the day before.

To prepare the aubergines, slice them finely lengthways, then fry in olive oil for about 3 minutes on each side; drain well on kitchen paper.

Remove the meat from the sauce with a slotted spoon, place in a bowl and season well with salt and pepper. Line six medium ramekins with aubergine slices, fill with lamb and cover with aubergine. If the meat seems to be dry, add some of the sauce to it. Put into the refrigerator until ready to heat. Season with salt and pepper to taste and strain the sauce. If you need to thicken it slightly, add a little brown roux (see tip opposite).

Prepare the couscous salad. Put the garnish tomatoes into an ovenproof dish and sprinkle with sugar.

When ready to eat, put the ramekins into an oven preheated to 150°C (300°F/Gas 2) for 20 minutes. Roast the tomatoes at the same time. Sear the lemon skins in hot oil for 2 seconds, and heat up the sauce.

Serve the tagine parcels turned out onto serving plates, with some couscous salad to the side. Put the preserved lemon skin on top of the aubergine, and the sauce around. Garnish with the tomatoes.

TIP:

A brown roux is wonderfully useful for thickening sauces. Depending on what it's needed for, you usually want equal quantities of butter and plain flour. Melt the butter in a small saucepan over a low heat, and then add the flour. Stir most of the time for about 15 minutes until it is a light chocolate brown. Allow to get cold and refrigerate until required.

Individual Steak and Kidney Puddings with a Root Vegetable Purée and Purple Sprouting Broccoli

For me this is good food at its best. A rich stew wrapped in pastry. The pastry in this recipe is a little different from what you might expect: hot-water crust instead of the usual softer suet pastry. You don't need any potatoes because of the pastry, but a couple of vegetables go well with it.

Serves 8

700g (1½lb) stewing steak, cubed
200g (7oz) ox kidney, trimmed and cut into small pieces
1 quantity Hot-Water Suet Crust Pastry (p.210)

Marinade
1 bottle red wine
1 small onion, roughly chopped
1 carrot, roughly chopped
1 celery stick, roughly chopped

Filling
2 tbsp olive oil
100g (3½oz) butter

2 tbsp plain flour
100ml (3½fl oz) brandy
4 bay leaves
1 tbsp chopped thyme leaves
1 garlic clove, chopped
salt and pepper
1 litre (1¾ pints) Meat Stock (p.207) or Chicken Stock (p.206)
1 tsp caster sugar

To serve
1 quantity Root Vegetable Purée (p.128)
1 quantity Purple Sprouting Broccoli with Lemon and Almonds (p.134)

Put the beef in a large container. Mix the marinade ingredients together, and pour it over the beef. Leave overnight. The next day remove the meat and the vegetables from the marinade and pat dry. Set aside. Keep the marinade wine.

Preheat the oven to 150°C (300°F/Gas 2). Seal the beef and kidney in a frying pan in a mixture of the oil and half the butter, browning the pieces on all sides. Transfer to a larger casserole. Wipe out the frying pan, melt some more butter and brown the vegetables all over. Add the flour and stir well, then decant into the casserole. Deglaze the frying pan with the brandy and add this to the meat as well. Boil the marinade wine to reduce by one-third and add to the meat with the bay leaves, thyme, garlic, some salt and pepper and enough stock to cover. Cook in the oven for about 2 hours, until the meat is tender. Remove the meat from the pot, strain the sauce through a fine sieve, add the sugar and mix well. Cool to allow the fat to rise to the top, then remove.

As soon as the pastry is made, cut into eight pieces. Roll out to circles about 23cm (9in) in diameter and use to line eight individual pudding basins. With your knife, cut around the edge at the top. With the little bits left from this trimming, mix to make tops.

Fill each of the lined basins to three-quarters full with some of the steak and kidney, and add a little of the juice. Cover with the rolled-out top, then fold over the top of the pastry lining the bowl. Seal well and cover with buttered greaseproof paper and foil, and tie up.

Put the puddings into a steamer and steam for an hour. (If you have two layers in your steamer, switch the layers around halfway through.) Meanwhile, prepare and cook the accompanying vegetables. Reduce the rest of the strained cooking juices until thick.

Turn out the puddings onto eight serving plates. Serve with the juices, the root vegetable purée and the purple sprouting broccoli.

Pork Tenderloin with Spinach, with Creamed Leeks, Garnished with Broad Beans and Crispy Celeriac

Pork, like chicken, is a white meat, and I feel it needs to be given flavours. The ginger really speaks through the dish, and makes it quite delicious, but then I like the combination of ginger and cream... The creamed leeks go particularly well too.

Serves 6

2 pork fillets, about 350g (12oz) each
salt and white pepper
olive oil

Creamed leeks
4 large leeks, cut into 1cm (½in) rounds
50g (1¾oz) unsalted butter
350ml (12fl oz) Chicken Stock (p.206) or water
3 tbsp crème fraîche
freshly grated nutmeg

Spinach stuffing
30g (1oz) butter

1 onion, very finely chopped
2 garlic cloves, chopped
2cm (¾in) piece fresh root ginger, finely chopped
2 tsp caster sugar
250g (9oz) cooked spinach, well drained and chopped

Garnish
1kg (2¼lb) broad beans in pod
200g (7oz) French beans
1 quantity crispy celeriac (see Crispy Vegetables, p.127)

First remove all the sinews from the pork, then cut each fillet across into three pieces and split each of these pieces lengthways without cutting through completely. Open out and carefully beat the six pieces of meat between pieces of cling film or greaseproof paper, until they are flattened to an even thickness.

To make the creamed leeks, sauté the leeks in the butter in a covered pan over a medium heat. Then add the stock and a pinch of salt and cook until very soft. Purée in a blender. Mix with the crème fraîche and season with white pepper and nutmeg to taste. Put to one side until ready to serve.

To prepare the spinach, melt the butter in a frying pan and soften the chopped onion for a few minutes over a medium heat. Add the garlic, ginger and sugar and cook for a further 5 minutes, then add the cooked spinach and mix thoroughly. Allow the spinach mixture to cool completely.

Preheat the oven to 180°C (350°F/Gas 4). Divide the spinach mixture between the six pieces of pork. Smooth out evenly, leaving a 1cm (½in) border all the way around on each. Carefully roll up the fillets and secure with string. Rub over with olive oil and season with salt and pepper to taste.

Sear the pork pieces on all sides in a large frying pan. Place on a baking tray and bake in the preheated oven for 8–10 minutes, until cooked through. Take out of the oven, cover with foil and allow to rest.

Pod the broad beans. Put them into boiling water for about 30 seconds, then refresh them in cold water. Pop the bright green centres out (a tedious job, but they look so pretty). Cook the French beans in salted water for a few minutes.

Cut each piece of pork into three and remove the strings. Place the pork on a plate, on top of the two types of beans. Garnish with the creamed leeks and top the pork with the crispy celeriac.

Medallions of Pork with Slow-roast Belly of Pork with Confit of White Cabbage

One of the most delicious things in the piggy world is belly of pork, but it is very fatty. Undoubtedly the tastiest meat is often the fattiest meat. This is one of those occasions when you forget about calories; just cook it, it's worth it. And with cabbage and greens, how could you get better than that?

Serves 4

1.5kg (3lb 3oz) belly of pork, skin finely scored
4 garlic cloves, finely chopped
salt and pepper
2 tbsp each of chopped tarragon and parsley
1 large pork tenderloin, sinews removed
1 large onion, finely sliced
4 large sprigs thyme
olive oil
200ml (7fl oz) Chicken Stock (p.206)

Greens
400g (14oz) spring greens
50g (1¾oz) butter

1 Granny Smith apple, cored and finely diced
2 garlic cloves, crushed

Sauce
75ml (2½fl oz) white wine
200ml (7fl oz) Chicken Stock (p.206)
100ml (3½fl oz) double cream
2 tbsp Dijon mustard

To serve
1 quantity White Cabbage and Caraway Seeds (p.136)
4 sprigs chervil

Preheat the oven to 150°C (300°F/Gas 2). Remove the excess fat from under the belly. Rub the belly with the finely chopped garlic and 1 tsp salt. Rub another 1 tsp of salt into the skin, making sure you get into those cuts (this helps the crackling along).

To prepare the pork medallions, mix the tarragon and parsley, and add some salt and pepper to taste. Cut the pork tenderloin across in half and cut the ends to make two neat pieces. Roll each piece in the herb mixture, then roll up tightly in cling film and refrigerate for 1 hour.

Put the sliced onion into a roasting tin with the thyme, and place the belly on top. Sprinkle with a little oil and pour the chicken stock in. Cook in the oven for 1½ hours, then turn the oven up to 190°C (375°F/Gas 5) and cook for a further 40 minutes. Allow to rest for 15 minutes.

Meanwhile, cook the cabbage (p.136) and the greens. For the greens, remove the stalks from the leaves, finely shred the leaves and blanch in boiling water for 1 minute, then drain and refresh. Make sure the greens are well drained. Melt the butter in a large

frying pan and fry the diced apple for 1–2 minutes. Add the garlic and the greens, and season with salt and pepper. Put the cabbage and greens to one side until needed.

To make the sauce, once the belly of pork is cooked and removed from the roasting tin, deglaze the tin with the white wine. Now add the chicken stock, mix well and strain into a small saucepan. Reduce a little. Add the cream and Dijon mustard, and season with salt and pepper to taste.

Remove the cling film from the pork fillet pieces carefully so as not to disturb the herbs. In a large frying pan add a little oil and fry the pork on a high heat until brown all over. Put into the oven for about 8 minutes.

Meanwhile heat through the cabbage and greens. Cut the belly of pork into slices and put on top of the greens. Cut each piece of pork into three, and put three medallions on top of the white cabbage, with sauce around. Put a piece of crackling on top of the pork, and garnish with chervil.

Venison Casserole, Venison Loin and Cabbage with Baby Currants

I offer no excuse for including three venison recipes. I use a lot, as we have our own very handy! This recipe would be suitable for a large number of people. It's not really necessary to have the two types of venison; you could simply have a helping of stew with some cabbage and mashed potato. While the casserole is cooking, you can prepare and bake your pastry boxes (there is a description of how to do this on p.56).

Serves 4

700g (1½lb) haunch of venison, boned and cut into 2.5cm (1in) cubes
olive oil
Game stock or Chicken Stock (p.206) to cover
salt and pepper
450g (1lb) Puff Pastry (p.210)
1 egg yolk, to glaze the pastry
450g (1lb) boned loin of venison, trimmed
25g (scant 1oz) brown roux (p.99)

Marinade
4 streaky bacon rashers, about 50g (1oz) in total, cut into lardons
1 small onion, roughly chopped
1 garlic clove, sliced
½ carrot, roughly chopped
1 celery stick, roughly chopped
1 bay leaf

1 sprig each of thyme and parsley
1 tsp each of coriander seeds and juniper berries, lightly crushed
1 tbsp olive oil
½ bottle red wine
100ml (3½fl oz) port

Mushrooms and shallots
2 tbsp olive oil
10 button mushrooms
10 shallots, peeled and left whole
1 tsp caster sugar
100ml (3½fl oz) red wine

To serve
1 quantity Cabbage with Baby Currants (p.135)
2 sprigs parsley, finely chopped

Toss the diced venison in a large non-metallic bowl together with all the marinade ingredients. Cover and leave it to marinate for several hours or overnight. Remove the meat from the marinade and pat it dry with kitchen towel. Reserve the marinade.

Preheat the oven to 170°C (325°F/Gas 3). Heat 1 tbsp of olive oil in a sauté pan and fry the strained meat until well browned. Tip the contents of the pan into a large casserole, and pour over the reserved marinade and all its contents. Just cover with stock. Season with salt and pepper to taste and stir well. Put the lid on the casserole and cook in the oven for 2 hours, or until the meat is tender.

Meanwhile, for the mushrooms and shallots, heat 1 tbsp olive oil in a clean sauté pan and fry the mushrooms for 3 minutes until any liquid has evaporated and they are golden. Remove from the pan. Add the remaining 1 tbsp of oil and sauté the shallots and sugar for 3–4 minutes until golden. Add the red wine and cook for about 10 minutes, until tender. Return the mushrooms to the pan with the shallots, season well with salt and pepper and reserve.

Now prepare the puff pastry for the top of the casserole. Roll, cut and chill, then glaze, cook and trim (as described in the scallop recipe on p.56). This can be done well in advance.

Once the casserole is out of the oven, increase the oven temperature to 180°C (350°F/ Gas 4). Set the casserole aside. Cut the loin of venison into two pieces. Heat a little olive oil in a frying pan and fry the loin quickly all over until evenly coloured. Transfer to the oven to roast for 8 minutes. Cover loosely with foil and leave to rest for 10 minutes.

Meanwhile, strain the cooked venison casserole through a sieve set over a clean pan. Reserve the venison, keeping it warm. Heat the casserole liquid over a medium heat. If it is not thick enough and it doesn't have enough body, stir in a little brown roux, allowing it to cook out before adding more, until the desired thickness is achieved. Return the venison to the sauce with the reserved mushrooms and shallots, and leave to heat through gently. (You can do all this the day before.)

To serve, carve each of the venison loin pieces into six slices and divide amongst the serving plates. Put a warmed pastry box beside this and spoon in some of the casserole. Put the pastry lid on top. Arrange some of the cabbage on the plate and garnish with parsley. Pour the sauce around.

Venison Loin with Beetroot, Black Pudding and a Juniper Sauce

When I was in Scotland, I cooked red deer, which was what was available – and the loins were huge – but at Swinton I only use fallow, which are very much smaller. I don't like my venison to hang too long, just a few days, as I prefer it fresh rather than too gamey. Whatever type you get, it's always better to undercook venison than overcook it. It's vital for this recipe to use veal jus, you need its texture to make a nice thick sauce that doesn't move on the plate.

Serves 4

4 pieces venison loin, each about 175g (6oz) in weight
olive oil
salt and pepper
4 x 1cm (½in) slices black pudding
20g (¾oz) butter

Juniper sauce
a few venison bones
35g (1¼oz) butter
1 tbsp olive oil
½ carrot, chopped

½ small onion, chopped
½ celery stick, chopped
100ml (3½fl oz) red wine
1 tbsp redcurrant jelly
250ml (8fl oz) Veal Jus (p.207)
1 tbsp juniper berries, lightly crushed
1 bouquet garni

To serve
1 quantity Grated Beetroot (p.132)
1 quantity Potato Galette (p.126)

Roll the venison in 1 tbsp of olive oil. Season with salt and pepper. Put aside for 1 hour.

Meanwhile, preheat the oven to 200°C (400°F/Gas 6) and make the sauce. Brown the venison bones all over in 15g (½oz) of the butter and the oil. Add the carrot, onion and celery and brown, then add the wine and redcurrant jelly and boil to a syrup. Add the veal jus, juniper berries and bouquet garni, and boil slowly until a little bit thicker. Strain into a clean pan and season well with salt and pepper.

Sear the venison all over in a little more olive oil, then put it in the oven for 4 minutes (if you have seared it ahead and let it get cold it will need an extra 2 minutes), or until it is still very springy but not soft. Let it rest for 5 minutes, covered with foil.

Fry the black pudding on both sides in the butter while the venison is resting. Reheat the beetroot and potato, as well as the sauce. Swirl the remaining butter into the sauce in small pieces.

Cut each piece of venison into three pieces, and place over the black pudding with a small pile of grated beetroot and a potato galette to the side. Pour the sauce around.

Venison en Croûte, Served with Red Wine and Port Sauce

This is a great party dish; it is lovely to do for a lot of people, and great for Christmas, as an alternative to goose or turkey. Its preparation requires a bit of concentration, and time, but the good thing is that you can prepare it, then freeze it. Just take it out the night before and let it defrost in the refrigerator.

Serves 4

1 piece loin of venison, about 600g (1lb 5oz) in total
olive oil
⅓ quantity Pancakes (p.198), you need 2 only
450g (1lb) Puff Pastry (p.210)
1 egg, beaten

Stuffing
2 shallots, very finely chopped
2 garlic cloves, finely chopped
a few knobs of butter
200g (7oz) wild mushrooms, finely chopped
100g (3½oz) button mushrooms, finely chopped
2 tsp thyme leaves
25g (scant 1oz) fresh breadcrumbs

salt and pepper

Sauce
bones from the venison
60g (2oz) butter
1 leek, finely chopped
1 shallot, finely chopped
1 bacon rasher, chopped
½ bottle red wine
3 tbsp redcurrant jelly
400ml (14fl oz) Game Stock (p.206)
300ml (10fl oz) port

To serve
1 quantity Juniper Cabbage (p.136)
1 quantity Celeriac Purée (p.127)

To make the stuffing, soften the shallots and garlic in some of the butter for a few minutes, then drain really well and leave to cool. Now soften all the mushrooms in a little more butter and then drain them in a sieve. We need the stuffing to be dry. When it is all cool, stir the onion and mushrooms together with the thyme and breadcrumbs and season well with salt and pepper. I sometimes add 1 tsp of very soft butter and mix it in with my hands. This moistens the venison.

Preheat the oven to 220°C (425°F/Gas 7). Season the venison pieces with salt and pepper to taste, then sear all over in hot oil. Let it cool for about 5–10 minutes.

Meanwhile roll out the pastry to a rough 30cm (12in) square, which should be able to wrap the meat like a parcel. It should be thin but still supple. Put the two pancakes on top of the pastry, slightly overlapping, and then top with the stuffing, making sure the pancake and stuffing will go all the way round the venison. Put the venison on top of that, right in the middle of the pancakes, and bring the pancakes up to meet at the top of the loin, where they will slightly overlap. You now have a pancake roll. So as to avoid

making a clumsy, pastry-heavy parcel, cut out and discard little rectangles from the four corners; it will look like a cross. Wrap it all up, first folding over the short ends and then the long sides. Seal with a little of the beaten egg. Turn upside down, with the join underneath, and place on a baking sheet. Brush all over with beaten egg.

Depending on the size of the en croûte, put into the oven for 30–35 minutes, turning halfway through. It will, and should, be rare.

During this time, prepare and cook the cabbage and celeriac.

For the sauce, brown the venison bones in half of the butter over a medium heat. Add the leek, shallot and bacon, and soften for a few minutes. Next add the wine and redcurrant jelly. Reduce this to a syrup and add the stock, reducing by half again. Finally, add the port before reducing it for the last time. Once it has reached a good consistency, finish it with the remaining butter. Season it with salt and pepper to taste, then strain it through a sieve.

Slice the venison and serve it with the vegetables and sauce.

Stuffed Saddle of Rabbit with Artichoke and Herb Risotto

We have thousands of rabbits at Swinton, and I can get as many as I want. They are tough as old boots, though, because they are wild, which is why I only use the loin. You could buy farmed and use the loin for this recipe, freezing the legs and making stock from the bones. Farmed rabbits have a much milder taste than wild, and their succulent flesh is much easier to cook than the tight-textured wild. This may be quite a fiddly dish, but it's a nice way of using some of that glut of rabbits...

Serves 4

4 rabbit saddles, each with 2 loins (order from your butcher)
salt and pepper
butter
150g (5½oz) large spinach leaves, blanched and separated, stalks removed

Mousse
2 globe artichokes
1 chicken breast, skinned and chopped
1 egg white
100ml (3½fl oz) double cream
1 carrot, very finely diced
60g (2oz) butter
1 tbsp each of finely chopped chives and thyme leaves
12 slices Parma ham

Sauce
bones from the rabbit saddles
olive oil
½ onion
1 carrot
2 bay leaves
1 sprig parsley
½ bottle white wine
1 tbsp redcurrant jelly
500ml (16fl oz) Chicken Stock (p.206)
100ml (3½fl oz) double cream
50ml (1¾fl oz) dry vermouth
a little white roux (optional, p.73)

Garnish
1 quantity Artichoke and Herb Risotto (p.22)
4 sprigs chervil

First bone the rabbit saddles and remove the loins. Cut down, following the bones around to take the loins off. You will have eight loins. (Or get your butcher to do this.) Reserve all the bones for the stock.

Next prepare the globe artichokes for the mousse, by first boiling them whole in salted water for about 25 minutes. Remove them from the water, allow to cool, then remove all the leaves down to the flower (the downy part in the centre). Scoop the flower away from the base of the artichoke with a teaspoon, then finely dice the artichoke bottoms.

To make the mousse, put the chicken breast in the processor and blitz. Add the egg white and process again, then gradually add the cream, using the pulse button. Put into a bowl and refrigerate.

Meanwhile gently soften the carrot in half the butter for a few minutes over a medium heat. Drain, then allow to cool. Add the remaining butter to the pan and toss the diced artichoke, chives and thyme until they are well coated. Drain, then season with salt and pepper to taste, and add to the carrots. Finally fold the cooled vegetables into the chilled mousse.

Take four double layers of foil, each about 35cm (14in) square, and butter each top layer. Put three slices of Parma ham onto each buttered piece of foil, lengthways towards you. Put two rabbit loins on the front of the sets of Parma ham, then season with salt and pepper to taste. Line leaves of spinach along the middle between each of the two loins, making a trench or channel for the mousse. Put your mousse mixture in the middle of each leaf, then wrap up the leaves to make long green sausages of mousse in the trenches between the pairs of loins. Make a lengthways incision along each pair of loins and spread the two wings around the spinach sausage on each. Then wrap everything up in the Parma ham, and then the foil. Put the parcels onto a tray in the refrigerator to settle for 1 hour.

Meanwhile, start making the risotto.

Preheat the oven to 200°C (400°F/Gas 6). When the rabbit is ready to cook, sear each parcel in the foil on each side in a dry pan, then roast in the oven for about 25 minutes, turning over halfway.

Meanwhile, make the sauce. Chop the bones into small pieces then sear them in a little oil in a large pan over a medium heat so they are very brown. Do not hurry this. Add the onion, carrot, bay leaves and parsley, and continue cooking for 10 minutes, then add the wine and redcurrant jelly, and simmer until it starts to thicken. Then add the stock and reduce to one-third. Strain through a fine sieve into a clean pan, add the cream and reduce for 3 minutes. Finish with the vermouth and season well with salt and pepper. Thicken with some white roux if necessary. Heat through when ready to serve.

Put some risotto into a bowl. Remove the foil from the rabbit parcels, slice each portion into three and arrange on the rice. Pour the sauce around. Garnish with chervil.

Vegetables and Accompaniments

easonal vegetables are the most exciting things. I look forward to asparagus in May and June, and eat as much as I can at that time. I look forward to spring greens too, and use them in many ways for the few short weeks they are around. To be honest, I look forward to everything...

Vegetables that are in season, are grown locally and that haven't had to travel too far will taste the best, will be freshest and will usually be cheaper. So it makes sense to buy them then, and enjoy them while you can. When the English asparagus season is over, I say goodbye – reluctantly, I must admit – but I wait quite happily for the next year. If you have a recipe that specifies something that is no longer around, don't buy expensive imported produce, look for a replacement. This means, in a sense, that you are making up your own recipe (what cooking is all about). None of the recipes in this book is written in stone, they are just guidelines. So if you can't find broad beans, find something similar or use frozen.

The classic British main course usually consists of meat and two veg. You won't find that in this book. The recipes here are for small vegetable or grain accompaniments, or vegetable and other garnishes – and there are a couple of salads too. Virtually none of my main-course recipes lacks a suggestion or two (sometimes even three!) of what I think would be a good vegetable or garnish to enhance the look and the flavour of the principal ingredient. Once again, if you can't find good spinach for a mousse, make something else: there are many recipes to choose from in this chapter. Many of the dishes here can actually be made all year round, as the ingredients are always on the shelves, but when the dishes are made with fresh produce they are especially delicious.

I don't always offer a carbohydrate, such as potato or a grain, but there are plenty of potato choices here, most of them classics. In fact I love all root vegetables, as there is so much you can do with them: you can boil, roast, sauté, purée and even deep-fry them. A crisp vegetable is a favourite garnish, and something like a parsnip purée with a parsnip crisp on top is packed full of flavour and texture. This is perhaps a theme of mine, serving a flavour or ingredient in more than one form (see my rhubarb recipes!), but of course you could just serve a vegetable purée on its own.

A number of the recipes here could be served as starters: the onion tarte tatin with a little goat's cheese on top, or the spinach or avocado mousse with a nicely dressed salad. Many of them would double as vegetarian dishes too. Even if you think some of the garnish suggestions would mean a lot more work, do remember that a fair proportion of them can be prepared in advance, and just heated through (if necessary) at the last minute.

Potato Fritters

Potato fritters make a good accompaniment and garnish to many main-course dishes. They are handy when you're rushed, as they can be done in advance and heated up in hot oil just before serving.

Serves 4

2 large floury potatoes (such as Maris Piper or King Edward), peeled and cut up small
20g (¾oz) butter
2 egg yolks and 1 egg white
2 tbsp very finely chopped parsley
salt and pepper
sunflower oil, for shallow-frying

Cook the potatoes in boiling water until tender, about 15 minutes, then drain well. Put them back in the pan to dry off over the heat. Now put them through a fine sieve. Add the butter and egg yolks, and mix well. Allow to cool. Whisk the egg white until foamy and fold it in too. Add the chopped parsley and season with salt and pepper to taste.

Heat the oil in a large non-stick frying pan. Drop spoonfuls of the potato, about four at a time, into the oil, and cook them in batches until golden brown, about 1 minute. Turn over when brown. Drain well.

Olive Oil Potato Purée

Instead of butter I have used olive oil in this delicious mash, which is good served with virtually anything. I put chopped sage into it, which is unusual, but you can obviously leave it out.

Serves 4

500g (1lb 2oz) floury potatoes (such as Maris Piper or King Edward), peeled and diced
130ml (4½fl oz) hot milk
2 tbsp chopped sage leaves
extra virgin olive oil
salt and pepper

Boil the potatoes in salted water until tender, about 15 minutes. Drain, then put through a coarse sieve. Gradually add the hot milk, then finally add the sage and olive oil; the latter needs to be done to taste. Season with salt and pepper to taste. You can prepare this quite a while in advance and leave to one side until ready to reheat.

Artichoke and Potato Purée

A potato purée with a difference, the potatoes being mashed with Jerusalem artichokes. The flavour is wonderful, and the combination is good with many fish and meat dishes.

Serves 4

250g (9oz) Jerusalem artichokes, peeled and diced
250g (9oz) floury potatoes (such as Maris Piper or King Edward), peeled and diced

50g (1¾oz) unsalted butter
at least 3 tbsp double cream
salt and pepper
freshly grated nutmeg

Bring two pans of salted water to the boil and cook the artichokes in one and the potatoes in the other for 15 minutes until tender. Drain well and mash separately before stirring them together. Add the butter and cream to the mash, beating well. Season with salt, pepper, and a little nutmeg to taste. Reserve, keeping warm, and reheat through to serve.

Mini Rösti Potatoes

This is a lovely way of doing a potato garnish, which looks very pretty with a variety of meat and fish dishes. The mini röstis can also be gently fried in a non-stick pan rather than baked in the oven.

Serves 4

2 large floury potatoes (such as Maris Piper or King Edward)

30g (1oz) unsalted butter
salt and pepper

Preheat the oven to 180°C (350°F/Gas 4). Peel and grate the potatoes, place on a cloth, and squeeze the water out of them. They should be as dry as possible. Mix them with the butter and salt and pepper to taste. Put a 6cm (2½in) ring on a baking sheet, and pack a layer of the potato in, about 1cm (½in) high. Remove the ring carefully, leaving a little round of potato on the sheet. Repeat this to make quite a few rostis.

Bake the röstis in the oven for about 30 minutes or until golden brown. Halfway through cooking, turn them over very carefully.

Fondant Potatoes

These luscious potatoes may take a long time to cook, but you'll be glad to hear they can prepared in advance. Put in a medium oven for 20 minutes to heat through.

Serves 4

4 waxy potatoes (such as Desirée), peeled   150ml (5fl oz) melted butter

Trim each potato into a rugby-ball shape, then cut off the top and bottom so they are equal sizes and flat at each end. Stand the potatoes on their ends in a small saucepan that will just hold the potatoes. Place the melted butter and an equal quantity of water (about 150ml/5fl oz) into the saucepan, just enough to come halfway up the potatoes. Simmer over a very low heat for half an hour, then turn the potatoes over and carry on until all the water and butter have evaporated. This should take about 1½ hours. Serve.

Parisienne Potatoes

These little balls of fried potato have a great flavour and texture. They are more a garnish than a proper accompaniment, but they make the dish look very pretty.

Serves 4

4 large waxy potatoes (such as Desirée)   salt and pepper
2–3 tbsp clarified butter (p.45)

Peel the potatoes. Use a melon baller to make balls of potato. Gently fry the balls in a little of the clarified butter over a low heat, moving them in the pan to coat them on all sides. Put the lid on for a short amount of time, but ensure the heat is really low. After about 15–20 minutes, remove the lid, move around again, and continue doing this until they are golden brown all over and cooked through. Season well with salt and pepper.

Rosemary Potatoes

These potatoes (named after the herb, not me!) are Italian in influence, and delicious with meat and poultry dishes particularly.

Serves 4

1kg (2¼lb) small, waxy potatoes (such as   olive oil
    Desirée)   coarse sea salt
1 rounded tbsp rosemary leaves

Preheat the oven to 180°C (350°F/Gas 4). Wash the potatoes and cut them into wedges, like large, blunt chips. Pound the rosemary leaves in a mortar, to release their flavour. Combine the potatoes and rosemary in a roasting tray, using enough olive oil to coat the potatoes. Roast for 1 hour, turning frequently. Season with coarse salt to taste.

Potato Galette

I use a Japanese mandolin for this, which cuts the potato into spaghetti strands, but you can use an ordinary mandolin. Slice the potato very, very finely, then cut by hand into very fine julienne, as thin as spaghetti.

Serves 4

1 large potato, peeled
salt

peanut oil

Put the potato onto a Japanese mandolin, and make into spaghetti strands. Season with salt to taste. In a small blini frying pan, heat a little peanut oil, and then place a few strands of potato in, leaving lots of gaps. Gently fry until golden brown. Carefully turn over – the strands will be sealed together by the potato starch – and brown the other side. Remove and put onto a tray very carefully, using a spatula.

Roasted Batons of Parsnips

The sweetness of parsnips is intensified by roasting; I also add some sugar here. They go well with many meat dishes. At certain times of year, parsnips get a little woody, when the centre or core is hard. If this is the case, cut that out too.

Serves 4

4 parsnips, peeled and cut into batons
olive oil

salt and pepper
caster sugar

Preheat the oven to 200°C (400°F/Gas 6). In a non-stick roasting pan, toss the batons in olive oil. Sprinkle with salt and pepper. Roast in the oven for about 40 minutes, turning over halfway through. Add a sprinkle of sugar 5 minutes before the end.

Celeriac Purée

You can make purées similar to this with any root vegetable. I would only use milk with a white vegetable, such as salsify, cauliflower, parsnip or fennel; it keeps them nice and white. Other vegetables don't need the lemon juice.

Serves 4

1 whole celeriac
lemon juice
1 small potato, peeled and diced

1 litre (1¾ pints) full-fat milk
60g (2oz) butter
salt and pepper

First peel the celeriac and put in some water with a little lemon juice to stop it from discolouring if not using it immediately.

Remove from the water and cut into rough 2cm (¾in) cubes. Boil with the potato in the milk, for about 20 minutes, until soft. When cooked, drain well. Put through a fine sieve and add the butter. Mix well, and season with salt and pepper to taste.

Alternatively, you could put the softened celeriac and potato into a processor, and then through a fine sieve (although this doesn't work with potatoes, which become starchy).

Crispy Vegetables

You can do this delicious and interesting-looking garnish with celeriac, parsnips, carrots, beetroot, potatoes, any of the root vegetables, and indeed pumpkin or squash as well.

Serves as many or as few as you like

root vegetable of choice
sunflower oil, for deep-frying

fine sea salt

Peel the root vegetable as appropriate. Take a potato peeler and finely slice down into ribbons. Or use a mandolin.

Preheat the sunflower oil to 170°C (338°F). Put the vegetable ribbons into the hot oil, a few at a time, and cook until golden brown, a few minutes only. Remove with a slotted spoon, and place onto some kitchen paper to soak up the oil. Season with fine sea salt to taste. Use as garnish.

TIP:

You can also use cabbage, which you treat in a slightly different way. Use large dark-green cabbage leaves – about eight to serve three – remove the tough stalks, and shred the leaves finely. Deep-fry in batches for 30–60 seconds until crisp. Drain and salt as above.

Glazed Baby Carrots and Onions

These baby vegetables are ideal for garnishing, and they look good too. I serve them with many meats, often with medallions of pork (p.105).

Serves 4

200g (7oz) shallots, with skins on
300g (10oz) young carrots
80g (3oz) unsalted butter, diced

1 garlic clove, finely chopped
1 sprig thyme
30g (1oz) caster sugar

Put the shallots into a saucepan and cover with water. Boil for 5 minutes, then drain and remove the skins. Put the shallots and carrots in a large pan with the butter, garlic, and thyme. Cook over a low heat, stirring often, for about 20 minutes, until the vegetables are tender. Add the sugar, then cook for 5 minutes. Season with salt and pepper to taste.

Roasted Shallots

This makes a great garnish. Shallots have so much flavour, and they are very versatile, accompanying many other vegetables and meats.

Serves 4

16 shallots
2 tbsp olive oil
a few sprigs of thyme

2 garlic cloves, roughly chopped
salt and pepper

Preheat the oven to 180°C (350°F/Gas 4). To peel the shallot so it does not fall apart, keep the root attached. Remove the outer skin, trying to keep the attractive shape. Put into a roasting tin with the olive oil, thyme, and garlic. Season with salt and pepper to taste. Roast in the oven for 35 minutes, moving them around in the tin about every 10 minutes.

Root Vegetable Purée

The one thing I think important about a vegetable purée is that it should be really fine, with no grain to it. It might be worth putting through a fine sieve.

Serves 4

200g (7oz) each of carrots, parsnips, and
   celeriac
2 garlic cloves
salt and pepper

60g (2oz) unsalted butter
100ml (3½fl oz) double cream
1 tbsp chopped parsley

Bring a large pan of water to the boil and cook the carrots, parsnips, and celeriac with the garlic for 10–15 minutes until tender. Drain well and process to a smooth purée in a blender. Season with salt and pepper to taste. Warm the butter and cream together in a clean pan and add the purée, mixing well to combine. Sprinkle with parsley. Serve warm.

Onion Tarte Tatin

This is a much more complicated recipe, and, although I usually serve it as a vegetable accompaniment, you could also use it as starter with perhaps a little piece of seared goat's cheese on top. It is great for a vegetarian.

Serves 4

250g (9oz) Puff Pastry (p.210)

Filling
about 100g (3½oz) butter
1 tbsp olive oil
2 large red onions, cut in half through
   the root

90g (3oz) caster sugar
1 tbsp red wine vinegar
150ml (5fl oz) red wine
1 tbsp chopped thyme leaves
2 garlic cloves, chopped
salt and pepper

Melt a third of the butter with all of the oil in a frying pan just big enough to hold the halved onions. Add the onions and brown all over a really low heat, which can take up to 20 minutes. Try not to hurry this. You will have to turn them a couple of times, but be careful that they don't come apart. Now add 40g (1¼oz) of the sugar, the vinegar, red wine, herbs and garlic, and season to taste with salt and pepper. Then cover and simmer for a further 30 minutes until the onions are very tender. Remove the onions from the pan, put onto a plate, and allow to cool. The small amount of liquid that is left should be very thick. If not, reduce down a little more, then put into a small saucepan ready to heat up later.

Preheat the oven to 200°C (400°F/Gas 6). Roll out the pastry until about 3mm (⅛in) thick. Cut it into four pieces: you want to make a circle from each that is about 2cm (¾in) larger than your little individual tart tins.

Melt half of the remaining butter in a small pan, with the remaining sugar, and mix. Butter the four small tart tins and put a spoonful of the butter-sugar in each. Top with a half onion, then put a circle of the pastry on top, tucking it in all round the edges.

Bake the little tarts in the oven for about 20 minutes, checking after 15. The pastry should be golden brown. Remove from the oven and allow to rest for a couple of minutes. Turn out and serve with a little of the onion sauce spooned on top to glaze.

Baby Leeks with Tomato and Herb Vinaigrette

These are incredibly simple to do. The vinaigrette can be made well in advance, and the leeks cooled at the last minute. They are delicious with individual fish pies, or any chicken dish. They can be served hot or cold.

Serves 4

12 baby leeks, trimmed
salt and pepper
extra virgin olive oil

Vinaigrette
200ml (7fl oz) extra virgin olive oil
1 small onion, finely diced
1 tbsp each of thyme and tarragon leaves
2 sprigs parsley

3 garlic cloves, roughly chopped
1 tbsp white wine vinegar
1 tsp freshly ground black pepper
2 tsp caster sugar
salt
6 tomatoes, skinned (p.146), seeded and
  finely diced
3 sprigs curly parsley, finely chopped

Preheat the oven to 180°C (350°F/Gas 4). Trim the baby leeks and put into a baking dish. Season with salt and pepper to taste, and drizzle with a little oil. Bake for about 40 minutes in the oven, turning over halfway through.

To make the vinaigrette, put the olive oil in a small saucepan with 1tbsp water and all the remaining ingredients apart from the tomato and chopped parsley. Bring up to heat and simmer for a couple of minutes. Put through a fine sieve, then add the tomato and chopped parsley. Serve with the leeks.

Roast Baby Beetroots

Beetroot is a favourite of mine, and I love these little baby ones, simply cooked in the oven. So simple, you just put them in and leave them there!

Serves 4

12 baby beetroot
1 sprig thyme

olive oil
salt and pepper

Preheat the oven to 150°C (300°F/Gas 2). Wrap the beetroot in foil with the rest of the ingredients so that it is airtight, and roast in the preheated oven for at least an hour, perhaps even another 30 minutes.

Grated Beetroot

An earthy dish, with plenty of flavours, this goes very well with red meats such as beef or venison, or wild duck such as mallard.

Serves 4

1 orange
4 beetroot
1 tsp chopped tarragon

2 tsp balsamic vinegar
60g (2oz) butter
salt and pepper

Cut julienne strips from the orange rind, preferably with a zester. Blanch the orange zest three times in boiling water for 1 minute each time.

Boil the beetroots for about 1 hour or until tender, then cool a little before skinning and grating coarsely on the coarsest grater you have. Next add the tarragon, vinegar, orange zest, and butter, and season with pepper and salt to taste. Reheat when ready to serve.

Buttered Baby Turnips

A real treat when they come into season, turnips are good with honey, too, or simply oven-braised, as here. Cook more if you want; I often cook more per person at home.

Serves 4

12 baby turnips
60g (2oz) butter

salt and pepper

Thoroughly clean the turnips, keeping the little green stalks on. Put the turnips into a pan of salted boiling water and cook until just tender. Then drain well and put into a separate pan with the butter, season with salt to taste, and brown on all sides until slightly brown.

Cauliflower Purée

Cauliflower gratin is a very comforting dish, but this purée is a great accompaniment to lamb, chicken, guinea fowl or boiled ham – anything in fact. Apart from game – funnily enough that combination just doesn't do anything for me.

Serves 4

1 large cauliflower
1 bay leaf
equal quantities of milk and water
60g (2oz) butter

25g (scant 1oz) plain flour
3 rounded tbsp freshly grated Parmesan
   cheese
salt and pepper

Cut the cauliflower into florets and put into a large saucepan with the bay leaf and enough milk and water to cover. Bring to the boil and cook for 15 minutes. Drain well.

In the same saucepan melt half the butter and add the flour. Mix well to make a roux (p.73), and cook for 1 minute. Put the cauliflower and the remaining butter into a blender and process until very smooth. Now tip the cauliflower into the saucepan with the roux, and mix well. Bring up to a simmer and cook until it becomes firmer. Stir in the Parmesan and season with salt and pepper to taste.

Purple Sprouting Broccoli with Lemon and Almonds

I look forward every year to the purple-sprouting-broccoli season, as I do to the other spring vegetables, like spring greens, asparagus, etc. They are all so delicious, and they look very pretty on the table too.

Serves 4

salt and pepper
450g (1lb) purple sprouting broccoli, stalks
   cut into 4
25g (scant 1oz) unsalted butter

juice of ½ lemon
25g (scant 1oz) sliced almonds
salt and pepper

Bring a pan of salted water to the boil and cook the broccoli until *al dente*. Drain well and keep warm. Meanwhile, melt the butter in a small pan and add the lemon juice and almonds. Cook slowly and stir constantly until the butter and nuts are a rich golden brown. Season well with salt and pepper. Pour over the warm broccoli, and serve.

Pea Pancakes

This recipe is incredibly useful, as you can have it either as a vegetable or as a little starter. It's a little drop scone really, but you could use it as an alternative for a blini, served with some good smoked salmon, a little caviar, and soured cream.

Serves 4

100ml (3½fl oz) full-fat milk
100g (3½oz) frozen peas
5g (¼oz) unsalted butter
1 rasher streaky bacon, finely chopped

2 tbsp plain flour, sifted
1 egg, beaten
salt and pepper
1 tbsp vegetable oil

Bring the milk to the boil in a small pan. Add the peas and cook for about 3 minutes until tender. Meanwhile, melt the butter in a small frying pan and sauté the bacon for 2–3 minutes until crisp and golden.

Process the peas and milk in a blender until smooth, then transfer to a medium bowl. Put the flour and eggs into a second bowl, and whisk to a paste. Fold in the pea mixture, then stir in the bacon and any fat from the pan. Season with salt and pepper to taste.

Heat the oil in a large crêpe pan and place eight spoonfuls of the batter mixture, set apart from each other, around the pan. Fry for 2–3 minutes on each side until cooked through and golden. They will pop up like a drop scone. Keep warm until ready to serve.

Cabbage with Baby Currants

You can use any currants, but I love those tiny ones from Greece, called Vostizza, which are virtually seedless. They are available from good delis or supermarkets. If you can't find them, go for ordinary currants and just chop them up a little.

Serves 4

1 Savoy cabbage
1 tbsp baby currants
2 tbsp warm Chicken Stock (p.206)
25g (scant 1oz) unsalted butter

1 small onion, finely chopped
1 garlic clove, crushed
100ml (3½fl oz) double cream
salt and pepper

Core and shred the cabbage. Cook the cabbage in boiling water for 1 minute, then strain well. Soak the currants in the warm stock for about 10 minutes.

Melt the butter in a large pan over a medium heat and sauté the onion and garlic for 2 minutes until softened but not taking on any colour. Add the cabbage, cover, and cook over a low heat for 2 minutes, tossing occasionally, until tender. Strain the currants and add them in halfway through. Stir the cream through, and season well with salt and pepper to taste.

White Cabbage and Caraway Seeds

This long-cooked cabbage is rather like a sort of sauerkraut. It may sound dubious, but it's delicious, especially with the caraway seeds. It's useful too as you can cook it up to two days in advance, and then just reheat when needed.

Serves 4–6

½ large white cabbage, finely shredded
½ bottle white wine
400ml (14fl oz) Chicken Stock (p.206)
1 tsp caraway seeds

150ml (5fl oz) double cream
1 tbsp caster sugar
salt and pepper

Put the cabbage into a saucepan with the wine, and bring to the boil for 2 minutes. Now add the stock and caraway seeds, cover, and cook for about 1½–2 hours until very soft, turning occasionally. Strain the cabbage, keeping the stock.

Add the cream and sugar to the stock, and reduce it until it has thickened and there is very little left. It needs to be reduced right down so that it just coats the cabbage, rather than drowns it. Mix with the cabbage and season with salt and pepper to taste.

Juniper Cabbage

The flavour of juniper is so very distinctive, and it turns simple cabbage into something divine. This side dish is a great enhancer of game, game sauces, and game accompaniments too.

Serves 4

1 Savoy cabbage
60g (2oz) butter
10 juniper berries, lightly crushed

1 garlic clove, chopped
salt and pepper

First remove the stalk from the cabbage, then shred the leaves and cook in boiling water for 30 seconds. Drain really well and refresh with cold water. Leave until ready to serve.

Melt the butter in a large sauté pan, add the cabbage with the rest of the ingredients and stir well to heat through. Season well with salt and pepper to taste.

Spinach Mousse

This is another of those vegetable accompaniments that could double as a first course, with something else on the plate. It can be eaten hot or cold. When there's a glut of spinach – as there usually is at Swinton Park – this is the answer!

Serves 4

250g (9oz) spinach, stalks removed
15g (½oz) unsalted butter, plus extra
  for greasing
1 egg

75ml (2½fl oz) double cream
pinch of freshly grated nutmeg
salt and pepper

Preheat the oven to 160°C (325°F/Gas 3). Cook the spinach in the butter in a large pan until wilted, and drain very well, squeezing dry if necessary. Liquidise the spinach and egg in a blender and then carefully add the cream, blending for a few seconds more. You will be in trouble if you over-process the cream, so be careful and use the pulse button. Season with nutmeg and salt and pepper to taste.

Pass the mixture through a medium sieve and divide between four buttered 100ml (3½fl oz) dariole moulds. Cover with foil, arrange in a deep baking tray and set aside until ready to cook.

Pour enough cold water into the baking tray to come most of the way up the sides of the dariole moulds, and transfer the *bain-marie* (double boiler) to the oven to cook for about 45 minutes until the mousses are cooked through.

Stuffed Courgettes

These make quite a substantial vegetable garnish – great with a lamb stew – but they could also serve as a lunch dish for two, served with a good salad. The stuffed courgettes can be prepared in advance and reserved until ready to bake.

Serves 4

3 large courgettes
2 tbsp fresh white breadcrumbs

Filling
3 tbsp olive oil
1 aubergine, very finely chopped
1 large courgette, finely chopped

2 garlic cloves, finely chopped
1 tbsp finely chopped thyme leaves
½ red pepper, skinned (p.23) and very finely chopped
2 tbsp finely and freshly grated Parmesan cheese
salt and pepper

Preheat the oven to 180°C (350°F/Gas 4). To prepare the courgettes for baking, cut each into four pieces about 3–4cm (1½in) in length. Using a melon-baller, carefully scoop the inside flesh out from one end of each piece of courgette, but without going through the opposite end, to make 12 little containers. Bring a pan of water to the boil and blanch the prepared courgette pieces for 1 minute. Remove and refresh in ice-cold water until cold, then drain them upside down on kitchen paper. Arrange the courgettes, standing vertically, open-side up, in a gratin dish.

For the courgette filling, heat 2 tbsp of the oil in a frying pan and sauté the aubergine for 3–4 minutes until soft. Remove and drain well on kitchen paper. Add the chopped courgette to the pan with the remaining 1 tbsp of oil and the garlic and thyme. Sauté for 3–4 minutes until just tender. Drain well on kitchen paper also.

Mix the aubergine and courgette together in a medium bowl with the red pepper and Parmesan. Season well with salt and pepper, then spoon this mixture into each courgette cavity. Sprinkle the breadcrumbs over the top.

Bake the stuffed courgettes for 20 minutes until they are warmed through and the crumbs are golden.

Avocado Mousse

This is a very simple and versatile accompaniment. You could make it in individual ramekins, which you would decant onto serving plates, or you could make in a big bowl, from which you would spoon out quenelles.

Serves 4

1 gelatine leaf
200g (7oz) ripe avocado flesh (about 2 pears)
50g (1¾oz) unsalted butter
50ml (1¾fl oz) lemon juice (about 1 lemon)

salt
good pinch of cayenne pepper
150ml (5fl oz) double cream, lightly whipped
½ tbsp finely chopped dill

Soak the gelatine in cold water. Purée the avocado. You need to work as quickly as possible to avoid discoloration.

Very gently heat a quarter of the avocado in a small pan, and add the butter, stirring all the time. Remove the pan from the heat, add the gelatine, without its water, and stir to make sure that it has all dissolved. Fold the gelatine mixture into the rest of the puréed avocado along with the lemon juice. Season well with salt and pepper, and fold in the whipped cream and dill. Do not over-whip the cream.

Spoon into four appropriately sized moulds lined with cling film. Place in the refrigerator for 4 hours. Carefully unmould the avocado mousse onto a platter, or use as a garnish.

Wild Mushroom Fricassée

This is a great accompaniment for a steak or chicken, but it would be lovely put into a little box of puff pastry (p.210), or on top of a plain risotto. In the latter guise, it would be a perfect dish for vegetarians.

Serves 4

1 large shallot, finely chopped
70g (2¼oz) butter
50g (1¾oz) shiitake mushrooms
2 garlic cloves, finely chopped
200g (7oz) wild mushrooms, sliced
70g (2¼oz) button mushrooms, finely sliced

3 tbsp Madeira wine
150ml (5fl oz) Chicken Stock (p.206)
1 tbsp each of finely chopped parsley and tarragon
100ml (3½fl oz) double cream
salt and pepper

In a large frying pan soften the chopped shallot over a low heat until translucent. Add the shiitake mushrooms and garlic and cook for 2 minutes. Now add the wild mushrooms and cook for a further 1 minute, then add the button mushrooms and cook for a further 5 minutes. Add the Madeira and reduce to a thick consistency. Finally add the chicken stock, herbs, and cream. Cook until you have a syrupy consistency. Season well with salt and pepper, then leave until needed.

Waldorf Salad

This is a very specific garnish for the Salmon Terrine (p.37), for which it is important that everything is cut up finely. You can, of course, cut it up less finely – then it is a more normal Waldorf, which would happily accompany simple grilled meat or fish.

Serves 4–8

1 Granny Smith apple
¼ fennel bulb
juice of 1 lemon
175g (6oz) seedless black grapes
2 tbsp Mayonnaise (p.217)
1 tsp plain yoghurt
olive oil
2 celery sticks, finely diced

salt and pepper
60g (2oz) walnut halves
2 Little Gem lettuces
½ frisée endive

To serve
best extra virgin olive oil
3 tbsp finely chopped dill

Core, peel, and finely dice the apple, and finely dice the fennel. Mix them together in the lemon juice to stop them discolouring. Halve the grapes and toss into the apple mixture.

In a large bowl mix the mayonnaise, yoghurt, the lemon juice from the apple mixture, and a few drops of olive oil. Now mix the apple, fennel, grapes, and celery into the mayonnaise, and season well with salt and pepper. Roughly chop the walnuts and toss them in. Chop the Gems into long strips and toss in at the last moment with the frisée. Garnish with a few drops of your best extra virgin and the dill.

Asparagus and Beans

At Swinton, we have rows and rows of asparagus, and I get so excited when it's time to cut it. There is so much, in fact, that we can't use it all up – rather like our baby artichokes. But what a combination that would be...

Serves 4

large handful of fine beans, topped and
    tailed
20 asparagus spears, hard ends removed

60g (2oz) butter
salt and pepper

Blanch the beans in boiling water for 3 minutes, then remove from the water with a slotted spoon. Drain, refresh, and dry the beans. Plunge the asparagus into the same boiling water for 1 minute then drain, refresh, and dry.

Cook the vegetables gently in the butter over a medium heat until tender, for a couple of minutes only. Season with salt and pepper to taste.

Ratatouille

This is my version of the southern French classic, which is such a useful accompaniment in summer, when all the ingredients are in season. By cutting everything quite small, I find you get more flavour.

Serves 4

3 red peppers
olive oil
1 small aubergine, finely diced
1 small onion, finely diced
6 large tomatoes (not beef), skinned (p.146), seeded and diced

2 large courgettes, finely diced
2 garlic cloves, finely chopped
handful of basil leaves
1 level tbsp tomato purée
salt and white pepper

Preheat the oven to 190°C (375°F/Gas 5). Roast the peppers until they start to blister, about 30 minutes, then remove from the oven and put into a plastic bag (this helps to steam the skin off). Allow to cool a little, then remove the skin. Seed the peppers, then cut them into small dice.

Heat a little olive oil in a large pan and cook the aubergine for a few minutes until softened. Drain in a colander. Using a little more olive oil each time, add the onion and soften, and now add the courgettes. Cook them for a minute, the drain them in the colander with the aubergines.

Add the tomatoes and garlic to the pan, and gently cook for about 5 minutes. Now add the basil and tomato purée, and cook until the sauce thickens. Add all the vegetables to the sauce, and cook gently for a further couple of minutes, mixing everything together. Season with salt and pepper to taste.

Braised Flageolets

I love braised dried beans, and flageolets are particularly delicious. They're good with many meats, but I like them best with lamb. Never cook dried pulses with salt at first, as this hardens their skins.

Serves 4

200g (7oz) dried flageolet beans
½ onion
1 bay leaf
1 tbsp olive oil
1 garlic clove, chopped

2 tomatoes, seeded and finely diced
500ml (16fl oz) unsalted Chicken Stock
　(p.206)
leaves from 1 sprig oregano
salt and pepper

Rinse the beans really well under cold water. Place them in a medium pan with the onion and bay leaf, and pour enough water over to cover by about 10cm (4in). Bring to the boil, reduce to a simmer, and cook for 1½–2 hours until tender, skimming any impurities from time to time. Drain well.

Heat the oil in a large sauté pan and cook the garlic for 1 minute. Add the tomato and the drained beans, with enough chicken stock to cover, and simmer gently for 15 minutes. Stir the oregano through and season well with salt and pepper.

Lentils and Pink Peppercorns

Lentils need a bit of a bite, so I have added pink peppercorns, which not only contribute flavour, but also add colour, making the dish look very pretty. This is a useful dish because it can be prepared the day before.

Serves 4

150g (5½oz) green lentils
1 onion, cut in half
at least 750ml (1¼ pints) Chicken Stock
　(p.206)
salt and pepper

2 shallots, finely chopped
1 garlic clove, finely chopped
15g (½oz) butter
240ml (8fl oz) double cream
3 tbsp pink peppercorns

Cook the lentils with the onion halves in enough chicken stock to cover over a medium heat until they are soft but not mushy, about 25 minutes. Do not strain. Add a little extra stock if needed. Season with salt and pepper to taste. Remove the onion and discard it.

Soften the shallot and garlic in the butter in a new pan over a low heat for about 10 minutes, then add to the lentils. Now stir in the cream and pink peppercorns, and put to one side. Season well with salt and pepper. Heat through when you are ready.

Couscous Salad with Lemon

Couscous is the traditional accompaniment to the Moroccan tagine, but this salad would be delicious with many other things – especially with meats grilled on the barbecue. I use the quick couscous, which saves hours.

Serves 8

200g (7oz) quick couscous
1 red chilli, seeded and very finely chopped
2 tbsp very finely chopped parsley
finely grated zest of 1 lemon
1 small red onion, very finely chopped
2 tbsp very finely chopped mint
10 green olives, stoned and finely chopped
  (optional)
4 garlic cloves, very finely chopped
4 tomatoes, skinned (see tip below),
  seeded, and diced
2 tsp freshly ground black pepper

3 tbsp very finely chopped chives
250ml (8fl oz) boiling Chicken Stock (p.206)

Vinaigrette
50ml (1¾fl oz) lemon juice
200ml (7fl oz) extra virgin olive oil
2 tsp clear honey
salt and pepper

Put the couscous into a bowl and add all the ingredients except for the stock. Mix well, then add the boiling stock. Stir and cover with cling film, and then leave to stand for about 10 minutes. Remove the cling film and stir well.

Mix the vinaigrette ingredients together, seasoning well with salt and pepper. Stir into the couscous to taste, as you may not need it all.

TIP:

To skin tomatoes, bring a pan of water to a rolling boil. Remove the green core of the tomato by inserting a knife down into the tomato at this point and scooping it out. Mark the skin at the opposite end of the tomato with 2 score marks with the knife. Drop the prepared tomatoes into the boiling water for 25 seconds. Remove and immerse immediately in icy water. The skin should peel away easily

Herb Pilaff

This is a wonderful accompaniment to the Fricassée of Chicken (p.73), but it also goes well with grilled meat, fish, and sausages – or indeed with a meat or fish casserole. It can also be used as a poultry stuffing (p.78).

Serves 8

1 small leek
1 celery stick, trimmed
1 small onion
60g (2oz) butter
250g (9oz) basmati rice

at least 300ml (10fl oz) hot Chicken
    Stock (p.206)
4 tbsp chopped chives
2 tbsp chopped parsley
2 tbsp chopped tarragon
salt and pepper

Preheat the oven to 180°C (350°F/Gas 4). Chop all the vegetables into very tiny dice. Melt most of the butter in a roasting tin and turn the vegetables in it, warming them through. Add the rice and continue turning everything together over a low heat for a couple of minutes. Pour in the hot stock and cover the tray with some greaseproof paper, letting it rest lightly on the surface of the pilaff.

Bake in the oven for about 20–25 minutes until the rice is tender and still slightly nutty, topping up with stock if it is drying too quickly.

When the pilaff is ready, take it out of the oven, and fold in the herbs. Season with salt and pepper to taste and melt in the remaining butter. Put into eight small moulds and turn out onto the serving plates.

Polenta Cake

I use these as an accompaniment to pork, but they would be lovely with any chicken dish or guinea fowl. They would make a good base for vegetables – wild mushroom fricassée, for instance. You don't need to include the sage, I just love the taste.

Serves 4–8

180g (6¼oz) instant polenta
750ml (1¾ pints) boiling Chicken Stock (p.206)

salt
handful of sage leaves, chopped
olive oil

Pour the polenta into the boiling chicken stock, stirring continuously (otherwise it will become lumpy). Over a low heat add some salt and the sage, and continue to stir vigorously until the mixture is very thick, about 5 minutes. Remove it from the heat and spread it flat in a Swiss roll tin (or similar), lined with cling film. Leave to cool and set.

Once the polenta is cool enough to handle, cut into any shapes you like and fry briskly in hot oil until crisp.

Pearl Barley Risotto

This makes a nice alternative to a risotto made with rice, although it obviously takes longer. I like it served with breast of chicken, but it could also accompany a plainly grilled piece of fish.

Serves 6

20g (¾oz) butter
2 shallots, finely chopped
1 leek, finely chopped
2 celery sticks, finely chopped
200g (7oz) pearl barley

at least 500ml (16fl oz) Chicken Stock (p.206)
150ml (5fl oz) double cream
2 tbsp chopped tarragon
salt and pepper
3 tbsp chopped chives

Melt the butter in a thick-bottomed pan, add the chopped vegetables, and cook gently for 5 minutes without browning. Add the barley and stir well. Now add the stock, cover, and cook gently until the barley is cooked and softened, and all the stock has been absorbed. This will take about 1 hour.

Add the cream and tarragon and cook for another 5 minutes. Season well with salt and pepper, and sprinkle the chopped chives on top.

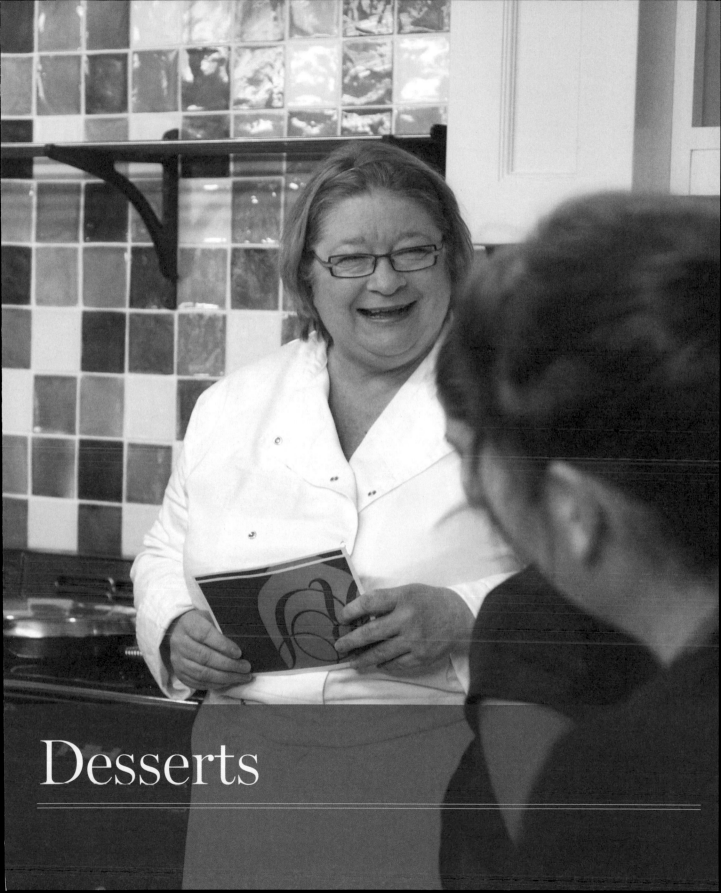

Desserts

I've never been a great pudding eater, but as I have grown older, my taste buds have changed. Now I like a little sweetness to finish off a delicious meal, and have even become a bit of a chocoholic...

Although for many people dessert is their favourite course, you don't need too much – you will have eaten two courses already, after all. Small is definitely beautiful here. I believe you should serve desserts in small, intensely flavoured portions. To make up for this miniaturisation, you could decorate the plate with any number of extras – sweet herbs such as mint, a spun-sugar cage (if you have the time and energy) or simply a scoop of ice cream or a crisp tuile. As with many of the recipes throughout the book, you can mix and match the garnishes and decorations to your heart's content.

All the chocolate recipes here are rather rich, so you don't need much. I favour a good dark chocolate with at least 70 per cent cocoa solids, and tend to buy this in small pieces known as *couverture pastilles* (which you can buy in good chocolate shops). These melt much more easily. If you can't find them, of course, do use a good dark block chocolate. The techniques involved in melting chocolate are rather too complicated to go into here, but basically, unless you are melting the chocolate with something else (butter or a liquor), it must never come in contact with direct heat; otherwise it becomes grainy and unworkable. To be safe, melt chocolate in a bowl that fits on top of a pan of simmering water without touching that water. This is the indirect heat with which chocolate is happiest.

Several tarts feature here – chocolate (pp.160–61), lemon (p.162), Bakewell (p.164) and classic French apple (p.175). A good home-made tart is a real treat, and my heart always lifts when I see one coming my way at a lunch or dinner party. Tarts are time-consuming to make – you have to blind-bake the case, make the filling, then bake the whole thing again – but many are served cold or need reheating only briefly when serving, so can be made well in advance. Do remember, though, to bake the fillings at a fairly low heat: anything with egg in it should be cooked gently. If you have the courage, take a tart out of the oven while the filling is still a bit wobbly; it will set as it cools.

Creamy puds need the same sort of care as creamy tart fillings. The classics here – crème caramel (p.165) and crème brûlée (pp.170–71) – should be baked at a low heat until they just wobble. Panna cottas – what I call two-minute wonders – are cold, creamy and set by gelatine rather than baking. My creamy ice cream (p.159) – a basic vanilla with a good selection of variations – is based on a creamy custard or crème anglaise. (I actually serve an ice cream or sorbet with almost every dessert!) The ultimate creamy, eggy dessert must be my Grand Marnier soufflé: I would advise practising this beforehand!

Chocolate Truffle Cake with Orange Confit and Coffee Crème Anglaise

When making this at the school, we sometimes put little spun-sugar trellises around the cakes, which look wonderful. Try if you have time, but remember, don't make them too far in advance, and don't put them in the refrigerator, as they go sticky. The orange confit makes a great garnish for many desserts, but you can also make it with lemons, when it would garnish savoury dishes.

Serves 8

50g (1¾oz) ground almonds
50g (1¾oz) caster sugar, plus 2 tsp extra
1 egg
1 tbsp melted butter
15g (½oz) unsweetened cocoa powder
2 egg whites
a little rum or Marsala (optional)

Chocolate truffle
220g (8oz) best-quality plain chocolate,
  broken into pieces
400ml (14fl oz) whipping cream
30g (1oz) icing sugar

Orange (or lemon) confit
2 oranges
75g (2½oz) caster sugar

To serve
1 quantity Coffee Crème Anglaise (p.214)

Preheat the oven to 200°C (400°F/Gas 6) and line a baking tray with baking parchment.

Start with the base. In a large bowl, combine the ground almonds, 50g (1¾oz) caster sugar, egg, melted butter and cocoa powder. In a separate bowl, whisk the egg whites to soft peaks, then add the extra 2 tsp caster sugar. Use a little of this mixture to slacken the almond mixture, then fold in the rest gently, so as not to lose too much air. Spread the mixture onto the baking parchment in a large rough circle. Bake for about 10 minutes until pale golden brown. Remove from the oven and leave to cool on the baking parchment until you are ready to use. It will not be crisp; more like a sponge.

When the sponge cake is cold, use eight stainless-steel 5cm (2in) mousse rings to cut out circles. Put the steel rings on a clean flat surface, with the sponge pieces at the bottom. If you like, you can brush them with a little rum or Marsala at this point.

For the chocolate truffle, melt the chocolate gently in a heatproof bowl set over a pan of simmering water. Whip the cream and icing sugar together just a little, so that the mixture will still pour, then whisk in the melted chocolate. Pour this on top of the sponge bases in the mousse rings, and even up the surface using a spatula, before putting in the refrigerator for 4 hours, or as long as possible.

Meanwhile, make the orange confit. Carefully peel the oranges, and remove and discard any pith. Cut the pith-free zest into fine julienne. Make a syrup with 100ml (3fl oz) water and the sugar, and simmer for about 3 minutes. Put the zest julienne in a small pan of boiling water and leave for 30 seconds. Strain and refresh with cold water, then repeat the process twice more. Now put the julienne in the syrup and cook for about 15 minutes. Keep an eye on it, as it is a very small quantity. Remove the julienne from the syrup, and leave to get cold.

Remove the rings, and put the little truffle cakes out onto individual plates. Garnish with some orange confit and a spoonful of coffee crème anglaise to the side.

Chocolate Terrine with Spiced Pears in Red Wine

This is a deliciously solid chocolate terrine, coated with finely chopped pistachios, and it's a useful recipe if you have to cater for quite a few people. The terrine itself will serve more than four (leaving you some for the next day), but if you have to serve more people than that, you could always halve the pears. As an added advantage, the terrine can be made well in advance.

Serves 4

300g (10oz) best-quality plain chocolate, broken into pieces
30g (1oz) icing sugar
300ml (10fl oz) whipping cream
70g (2oz) pistachio nuts, skinned and finely chopped

Pears in red wine
4 small whole pears
1 bottle good red wine

250g (9oz) caster sugar
2 pieces orange peel
juice of 1 lemon
1 cinnamon stick
2 bay leaves
2 cloves
2 tsp coriander seeds

Line a 450ml (15fl oz) terrine with cling film.

Melt the chocolate gently in a heatproof bowl set over a pan of simmering water (see p.153). Gently whip the icing sugar into the cream so that the cream will still pour, then whisk in the melted chocolate. Pour the chocolate cream mixture into the lined terrine and, using a spatula, smooth the surface until it is even, before putting the terrine into the refrigerator for at least 6 hours.

When the terrine has set, remove from the mould and carefully set on a board right-side up. Remove the cling film and press the chopped pistachios all over the top and sides. Wrap carefully in another piece of cling film and put in the refrigerator until needed.

To make the pears in red wine, peel the pears carefully, keeping the stalks on. Put all the ingredients, including the pears, in a large pan. Bring to the boil, then reduce the heat slightly and simmer for about 15 minutes. Remove the pears and boil the liquid hard until syrupy. Allow to cool, then pour over the pears.

Serve a pear per person, along with some of the strained juices, with slices of terrine.

Chocolate Profiteroles with Warm Chocolate Sauce

Everyone loves profiteroles with chocolate sauce, but the one big mistake everyone seems to make with profiteroles is not drying them off properly. Don't miss out that drying out at a low heat. Profiteroles freeze like a dream, before they're filled, so you could always have some ready to serve. I like this dish served with vanilla ice cream.

Serves 8

1 quantity Choux Pastry (p.211)
1 quantity Crème Pâtissière (p.214)
100ml (3½fl oz) whipping cream

Rich chocolate sauce
150g (5½oz) dark chocolate, broken
   into pieces
25g (scant 1oz) unsalted butter

150ml (5fl oz) double cream
1 tbsp golden syrup

To serve
8 sprigs of fresh mint
icing sugar, to dust
1 quantity Vanilla Ice Cream (see opposite)

Preheat the oven to 220°C (425°F/Gas 7). Have ready a baking mat or put a piece of greaseproof paper on a baking tray.

Make the choux pastry first. Put the choux mixture into a piping bag and pipe small balls, the size of a walnut, onto the mat or paper on the tray. Be careful not to pipe too close together, as they will expand to double in size. Bake in the oven for about 20 minutes, then reduce the oven temperature to 140°C (275°F/Gas 1) and leave for a further 20 minutes or until dried out. Allow to cool before filling.

Make the crème pâtissière and allow to cool.

To make the rich chocolate sauce, in a bowl, melt the chocolate and butter together gently (see p.153). Put the cream and golden syrup in a small saucepan and bring to the boil, mixing well. Now mix the cream into the chocolate and keep warm until you are ready to serve.

When ready to fill the choux profiteroles, first whisk the 100ml (3½fl oz) whipping cream to soft peaks, then add to the crème pâtissière and fold in well. Spoon into a piping bag with a fine nozzle. Using a skewer or something similar, make a small hole at the bottom of each profiterole, and pipe some crème pâtissière into each one.

To serve, put four or five profiteroles in the middle of each serving plate. Pour over the warm chocolate sauce and garnish with mint and a dusting of icing sugar. Add a scoop of home-made vanilla ice cream (if using).

Vanilla Ice Cream

This is my basic ice-cream recipe, which has as its base a doubled recipe of my crème anglaise (p.214), with the addition of double cream. It is very luscious, and can be varied in a number of ways (see below).

Serves 8 | **2 quantities Crème Anglaise (p.214)** | 150ml (5fl oz) double cream

Make the crème anglaise as described on p.214. When cool, add the cream (and any flavouring if making flavoured ice cream).

It is now ready to go into the ice-cream machine and be churned according to the manufacturer's instructions. If you don't have one – and I think they are such a good thing for those of us who like to make desserts – put the mixture in a suitable container and into the freezer. You will have to stir occasionally to prevent crystals forming.

Remember to allow a little time for the ice cream to soften slightly and reach edible temperature after coming out of the freezer, about 5 minutes.

Whisky, Calvados, or Grand Marnier Ice Cream Add 50ml (1¾fl oz) spirit.
Nougat Ice Cream See pp.166–68.
Pistachio Ice Cream Add 4 tbsp ground pistachio nuts (skin before grinding).

TIP: *Vanilla sugar is easy to make, and it adds such incredible flavour to so many desserts. Even when they have been split and used for something, the pods still have a lot of flavour. Simply put a rinsed and thoroughly dried vanilla pod inside a jar of caster sugar, and leave for at least a month. The sugar becomes permeated with the scent of the vanilla, and the pod can be used again in something else.*

Warm Chocolate Tart with Whisky Ice Cream

Chocolate and whisky are wonderful companions, and this is a great dessert, particularly for chocoholics. If you like, you could make individual tarts (see the recipe on p.186 for some ideas).

see the recipe on p.186

Makes
1 x 23cm
(9in) tart,
to serve 8

1 Sweet Tart Pastry Case (pp.212–13)
8-10 sprigs of fresh mint

Filling
150g (5½oz) butter
150g (5½oz) dark chocolate, broken
 into pieces

1 medium egg
3 medium egg yolks
60g (2¼oz) caster sugar

To serve
1 quantity Whisky Ice Cream (p.159)

Preheat the oven to 150°C (300°F/Gas 2).

To make the filling, melt the butter and chocolate together carefully in a heatproof bowl set over a pan of simmering water (see p.153). Whisk together the eggs, egg yolks and sugar just to combine. Now fold the chocolate mixture into the egg mixture, and pour into the pastry case.

Bake in the oven for about 30 minutes. Check the tart, as it may need a little longer. It needs to be smooth and creamy. It almost needs a slight wobble factor, just setting. Remove from the oven and leave to rest for 30 minutes in a warm place.

Serve the warm chocolate tart cut into wedges accompanied by the whisky ice cream and a sprig of mint.

Lemon Tart with Lemon Sorbet

Another example of my liking one particular flavour in more than one form: this is very much for lemon lovers, with the intense lemon filling in the tart matched by the lemon flavour of the sorbet.

Makes
1 x 23cm
(9in) tart,
to serve 8

1 Sweet Tart Pastry Case (pp.212–13)

Lemon filling
5 eggs, plus 1 extra egg yolk
180g (6oz) caster sugar
finely grated zest and juice of 3 lemons
150ml (5fl oz) double cream

To serve
1 quantity Raspberry Coulis (p.182) or
   Crème Anglaise (p.214)
1 quantity Lemon Sorbet (see opposite)

Preheat the oven to 140°C (275°F/Gas 1).

Make this tart in a 23cm (9in) tin, preferably 3.5cm (1¼in) deep. To make the lemon filling, whisk together the eggs, extra egg yolk and sugar in a large bowl. Now add the zest and lemon juice, then the cream, and whisk well for a moment or two. Leave to infuse until the tart case is cool. Strain through a fine sieve.

Once the pastry tart case has cooled, pour in the lemon mixture and bake in the oven for about 30 minutes until it is nearly set, and has that wonderful wobble.

Serve in wedges, garnished with raspberry coulis or crème anglaise to taste.

Lemon Sorbet

This sorbet is made in an unusual way. I use Italian meringue, which makes it better because the egg white is minimally heated, giving it a bit of body. It is lovely with lots of desserts, but particularly the lemon tart opposite.

Serves 6

100g (3½oz) caster sugar
finely grated zest and juice of 2 lemons

Italian meringue
130g (4¾oz) caster sugar
3 egg whites

Bring the sugar and 150ml (5fl oz) water to the boil in a small, heavy saucepan, stirring throughout. Reduce the heat slightly, simmer for 2 minutes, then remove from the heat and allow to cool. Add the lemon juice and zest to the syrup. Leave to infuse until cold, then strain through a fine sieve. Keep in the refrigerator until required.

To make the Italian meringue, put 2 tbsp water in a small, heavy saucepan and add the sugar. Using a sugar thermometer to measure the temperature, bring the liquid up to the boil. Keep brushing the sides of the pan with a wet pastry brush to stop the sugar from crystallising. Once the temperature has reached 110°–120°C (230°–248°F), or soft-ball stage, remove the pan from the heat. In a clean, dry bowl, whisk the egg whites until soft peaks form, and slowly add the warm sugar syrup, whisking continuously until the mixture is smooth and has cooled. Mix in the chilled lemon syrup.

To finish the sorbet, churn the mixture in an ice-cream machine according to the manufacturer's instructions, transfer to a suitable container and keep in the freezer until needed. Alternatively, pour the mixture into a suitable freezerproof container and put directly in the freezer. If using this method, remove the sorbet from the freezer every now and again as it freezes, over about 4 hours, and give it a stir to break down the crystals. Serve straight from the freezer.

Bakewell Tart

Bakewell tart, a sweet tart pastry base with an eggy almond cream filling, is a classic English dessert. When making Bakewell tart, you want a lattice of pastry on the top, so remember to save the trimmings of the pastry when making the pastry case.

Makes
1 x 23cm
(8in) tart,
to serve 8

1 Sweet Tart Pastry Case (pp.212–13), plus the pastry trimmings from making the case (wrap in cling film and chill)
1 egg yolk, to glaze

Almond cream filling
4 eggs, plus 1 extra egg yolk
120g (4½oz) caster sugar
150g (5½oz) butter, melted and cooled
120g (4½oz) ground almonds
1 tsp vanilla extract
about 150g (5½oz) raspberry jam, sieved

Preheat the oven to 150°C (300°F/Gas 2).

To make the almond cream filling, thoroughly mix together the eggs, egg yolk and sugar, then mix in the melted butter, ground almonds and vanilla extract.

Spread about 5 to 6 tablespoons raspberry jam on the base of the pastry case, top with the almond cream filling and bake in the oven for 40 minutes until the filling is slightly coloured and a skewer inserted in the centre comes out clean. Remove from the oven and allow to cool completely.

Now make a lattice by first rolling out the pastry trimmings very thinly, then use a lattice cutter to make the tart's pastry top. Carefully place the latticed pastry on top of the tart and seal at the edges. If you don't have one of these cutters, cut the pastry into thin strips and arrange on top of the tart to make a lattice pattern. Brush the top of the pastry with the egg glaze, and return to a preheated 150°C (300°F/Gas 2) oven for about 15 minutes until golden.

Remove the tart from the oven and allow to cool again. Put the rest of the jam in the holes in the lattice. Serve cut in wedges.

Coffee Crème Caramel with Coffee Tuiles

I love crème caramel and, of course, if you wanted a plain crème caramel, you would simply leave out the coffee flavourings. Here, the crisp coffee-flavoured tuiles provide the perfect complement to the smooth, creamy custard.

Serves 4

200ml (7fl oz) double cream
200ml (7fl oz) whipping cream
1 tbsp coarsely ground coffee beans
2 tsp instant coffee granules
3 eggs, plus 2 extra egg yolks
80g (2½oz) caster sugar
2 tsp vanilla extract

Caramel
250g (9oz) caster sugar
2 tbsp water

To serve
1 quantity Coffee Tuiles (p.202)

Preheat the oven to 150°C (300°F/Gas 2), and have ready four medium ramekins or moulds inside a deep roasting tin.

To make the caramel, dissolve the sugar with 2 tbsp water in a heavy saucepan over a low heat. Bring up the heat, and cook until the sugar turns a light caramel, being very careful not to let it colour any further. Carefully pour into the ramekins or moulds, and swirl around until the insides are coated.

Gently heat the cream and milk together with the ground coffee, just to simmering point, then turn off the heat. Allow to infuse as long as possible, then strain through a fine sieve and bring to the boil again. Remove the pan from the heat and stir in the instant coffee until dissolved.

Whisk together the eggs, extra egg yolks, sugar and vanilla in a small bowl, then mix into the cream and milk. Pour into the caramel-glazed ramekins.

Carefully pour enough cold water into the roasting tray to come halfway up the sides of the ramekins, to make a *bain-marie*. Bake the crème caramels for 25–30 minutes until completely stiff. If the water in the tin needs topping up, use cold water.

Remove from the oven and leave to cool thoroughly before turning out. Serve as they are with some deliciously crisp coffee tuiles.

Iced Nougat Parfait with Strawberries and Peach Coulis

This is an ice cream made rather like the sorbet (p.163), with an Italian meringue base. This means that the mixture doesn't freeze completely, so it always has that slightly unctuous soft texture. It's delicious with the crisp nuts throughout, and finished off perfectly with the sweet strawberries and their peach coating. The peach coulis could be made with many other fruits – try pineapple, for instance.

Serves 4

Nougat
100g (3½oz) flaked almonds
100g (3½oz) caster sugar

Meringue
150g (5½oz) caster sugar
3 egg whites
300ml (10fl oz) double cream

Peach coulis
250g (9oz) fresh peaches, stoned
juice of 1 lemon
1 tbsp sugar syrup (see tip p.168)

To serve
250g (9oz) ripe, sweet strawberries
2 tbsp icing sugar
½ lemon

Have ready four ramekins or one large terrine dish lined with cling film.

Toast the flaked almonds until golden brown by spreading them over a baking sheet and grilling them or heating them in a dry non-stick pan. Be careful not to let them scorch.

Put the caster sugar for the nougat in a saucepan and add 1½ tbsp water. Heat gently until all of the sugar has dissolved. Now increase the heat and cook until the liquid is a light caramel in colour, being careful not to overcook it or allow it to turn dark. Remove from the heat and mix in the toasted almonds, stirring with a wooden spoon until the almonds are completely covered. Turn the almond mixture out onto some oiled baking parchment or a baking mat, and allow to cool for 1 hour. Once cool, crush into tiny pieces using the end of a rolling pin.

To make the meringue, gently heat the sugar in a small pan until melted. Increase the heat, and test the temperature with a sugar thermometer. When it has reached 110°C (230°F), start whisking the egg whites in a bowl. When the egg whites form soft peaks, add the heated sugar slowly, whisking all the time, until the meringue mixture has cooled. (Do not stop whisking until cool.)

Now add the crushed sugared almonds to the meringue mixture. Whip the double cream to form soft peaks, and gently fold into the mixture. Put the mixture in the ramekin dishes or terrine and freeze for at least 6 hours.

Meanwhile, to make the peach coulis, simply purée the fruit and the lemon juice in a blender, pass through a fine sieve and add the cold sugar syrup. The strawberries just need to be finely diced and tossed with the icing sugar and a squeeze of lemon.

TIP: *To make a basic sugar syrup that is useful in a number of dessert dishes, bring 100g (3¹/₂oz) caster sugar and 100ml (3¹/₂fl oz) water to the boil to melt the sugar, stirring continuously throughout. Simmer for 2 minutes, then remove from the heat and allow to cool. Keep in the refrigerator until required.*

Baked Peaches with Amaretto, Ciambella and Pistachio Ice Cream

Known as *pesche all'amaretto* in Italy, these delicious peaches are baked in the oven with crushed amaretti – macaroons to us – and the almond liqueur Amaretto, then topped with whipped cream. This is a lovely summer dessert, especially when it is served with the luscious Italian cake ciambella – which has a hole in the middle – and pistachio ice cream.

Serves 4

6 peaches, halved and stoned
2 tbsp vanilla sugar (see p.159)
6 small amaretti biscuits, crushed
150ml (5fl oz) Amaretto (almond liqueur)

Lemon and orange ciambella
100g (3½oz) unsalted butter, melted
300g (10oz) plain flour
2½ tsp cream of tartar
1 tsp bicarbonate of soda

175g (6oz) caster sugar
2 eggs
finely grated zest of 2 lemons
finely grated zest of 1 orange
4 tbsp Vin Santo or other sweet white wine

To serve
1 quantity Pistachio Ice Cream (p.159)

Preheat the oven to 190°C (375°F/Gas 5). Brush the inside of a 22cm (9in) ring tin with a little melted butter, then dust with flour, tipping out any excess.

Make the ciambella first. Mix the melted butter, flour, cream of tartar, bicarbonate of soda and caster sugar in bowl. Now fold in the eggs, lemon and orange zests and wine. Mix well, but do not beat, as this will make the cake explode in the oven. (Ciambella is meant to be a firm cake.) Bake in the oven for 30 minutes or until a skewer comes out clean. Remove from the oven, turn out of the tin and leave to cool on a wire rack.

Reduce the oven temperature to 180°C (350°F/Gas 4). Put the peaches in a buttered ovenproof dish, cut side up. Sprinkle over the vanilla sugar and amaretti, then pour the Amaretto around the peaches. Bake in the oven for 15 minutes.

Serve the peaches warm with a slice of ciambella and a scoop of pistachio ice cream.

Passionfruit Crème Brûlée with Orange Sorbet

This is to die for. If you like, you can buy passionfruit purée from a good deli – much easier than trying to get enough basic material from passionfruits you open yourself. If you can't find it, you can use mango purée instead.

Serves 4

Orange sorbet
125g (4½oz) caster sugar
1 tbsp liquid glucose
500ml (16fl oz) fresh orange juice
1 tbsp Cointreau

Brûlées
1 vanilla pod, slit lengthways and seeds
  scraped out (keep the pod)

300ml (10fl oz) double cream
4 egg yolks
150g (5½oz) caster sugar
100ml (3½fl oz) passionfruit purée

Garnish
pulp of 4 passionfruit
fresh mint leaves

To make the sorbet, pour the sugar, glucose and 125 ml (4fl oz) water into a medium pan. Bring to the boil, stirring continuously. Reduce the heat to a simmer for 2 minutes, then remove from the heat and let cool. Stir the orange juice and Cointreau together in a large bowl. Add the cooled syrup, a little at a time, using enough to sweeten to taste.

Pour the mixture into an ice-cream machine; churn according to the manufacturer's instructions until beginning to freeze. Scrape out the sorbet into a suitable container with a lid and transfer to the freezer to set completely. (Alternatively, simply freeze the mixture in a suitable container, stirring every so often to avoid crystals forming.)

To prepare the brûlées, preheat the oven to 140°C (275°F/Gas 1). Add the vanilla seeds and pod to a medium pan with the cream and bring slowly to the boil. Remove from the heat and set aside. Whisk together the egg yolks and 50g (1¾oz) of the sugar in a large bowl until thick and pale. Slowly strain the cream into the egg mixture, whisking all the time. Don't whisk too much; you don't want it to be frothy. Mix in the passionfruit purée.

Arrange six small ramekins in a deep roasting tin. Pour the brûlée mixture into a jug and from this fill the ramekins to the top. Carefully transfer the tray to the oven, then pour in enough cold water to come halfway up the sides of the ramekins, creating a *bain-marie*. Bake the brûlées in the oven for 50 minutes or until just set. Remove the brûlées from the *bain-marie*, set on a baking sheet and leave to cool.

Preheat the grill to high. Sprinkle the remaining 50g (1¾oz) sugar evenly over the brûlée tops and grill for 1–2 minutes until the sugar has melted to a golden caramel, which sets to a crisp crust. Put a brûlée on each serving plate. Serve with a scoop of orange sorbet, garnished with some extra passionfruit pulp and fresh mint sprigs.

Grand Marnier Soufflés

I think this is one of the best hot soufflés, on a par with raspberry soufflé. It's a great winter pudding, very celebratory, and tastes intensely orange because of both the orange juice reduction and the orange liqueur. It is really important to reduce the orange juice thoroughly, as described.

Serves 4

2 tsp unsalted butter, for greasing
1½ tbsp caster sugar, plus extra, to sprinkle
250ml (8fl oz) freshly squeezed orange juice
4 rounded tbsp Crème Pâtissière (p.214)
2 tbsp Grand Marnier

4 egg whites
icing sugar, to dust

To serve
1 quantity Grand Marnier Ice Cream (p.159)

When ready to eat – and you must all be sitting ready for this – preheat the oven to 190°C (375°F/Gas 5). Butter the inside of four 7–8-cm (3–3¼-in) ramekins, 4–5cm (1¾–2in) deep, and sprinkle with a little caster sugar. Shake out any excess.

Put the orange juice in a saucepan over a medium heat, and reduce – please, it's important – to 2 tbsp. Now mix together the crème pâtissière, reduced orange juice and Grand Marnier.

Put the egg whites in a clean, dry bowl and whisk until soft peaks form. Add the 1½ tbsp caster sugar, and continue whisking for a few seconds until the mixture holds firm peaks. Whisk a third of the egg whites into the crème pâtissière mixture to loosen the mixture, then fold in the rest.

Fill the prepared ramekins, smooth the tops with a palette knife, and run your thumb around the edges of each one (which helps the rising). Cook the soufflés in the oven for about 8 minutes. Remove and dust with icing sugar. Serve immediately with some Grand Marnier ice cream.

Cold Passionfruit Soufflés with Mango Coulis

This soufflé mixture makes more than enough for eight people, and so there will be a little left over, but it's difficult to make less. These little soufflés are delectable, but then I have a passion for passionfruit. You can make these soufflés in winter, even though they are cold, not hot. They can also be made successfully for large parties, as everything is done in advance.

Serves 6

Soufflé
2 gelatine leaves
250ml (8fl oz) passionfruit purée (buy in good delicatessens)
130g (4½oz) caster sugar
3 egg whites
130ml (4½floz) double cream, lightly whipped

Garnish
pith-free zest of 2 oranges, cut in julienne
8 sprigs of fresh mint
8 small sprigs of redcurrants

Mango coulis
1 mango, peeled, stoned and puréed
juice of 2 oranges
1–2 tbsp sugar syrup (see p.168)

Wrap the outsides of six 6cm (2⅓in) ramekins with greaseproof paper to come 5cm (2in) above the rim. Tie on with string, or use sticky tape.

Blanch the orange zest for the garnish three times in boiling water, drain and set aside. Mix the mango coulis ingredients together and set aside.

To start the soufflés, soak the gelatine in a bowl of cold water for 15 minutes. Warm 2 tbsps of the passionfruit purée in a small pan. Squeeze the gelatine to get rid of excess water, add to the pan of warmed purée and stir until completely dissolved. Pour in the rest of the passionfruit purée. Set aside, stirring the purée occasionally, to prevent it from setting.

To make the Italian meringue, put 2 tbsp cold water in a pan and add the caster sugar. Heat gently, stirring until the temperature reaches 110°–120°C (230°–248°F), or soft-ball stage, on a sugar thermometer, brushing down any sugar crystals that form around the sides of the pan with cold water. Remove from the heat. Whip the egg whites to soft peaks. Add the sugar syrup very slowly, whisking all the time, for 5 minutes until very smooth. Whisk a third of the meringue into the passionfruit purée, then fold in the rest, followed by the cream. Spoon the mixture into the ramekins to come about 3cm (1¼in) above the rims. Chill for about 3 hours.

To serve, carefully take the paper away from the soufflés. Put the ramekins onto serving plates and decorate with the prepared orange zest. Put a small pool of coulis around the edge of each ramekin.

Prune, Armagnac and Cinnamon Tart with Chantilly Cream

This is a classic French tart, using two of the ingredients for which France is so famous – prunes and Armagnac brandy. The best prunes to use are the French Agen variety. These are pre-soaked and quite large, so you may not need to use so many.

Makes
1 x 23cm
(9in) tart,
to serve 6

1 x 23cm (9in) Sweet Tart Pastry Case
  (pp.212–13)

Filling
30 pitted prunes
Armagnac, to cover
75g (2½oz) butter, softened
75g (2½oz) ground almonds
75g (2½oz) icing sugar

2 eggs
30g (1oz) plain flour
1 tsp ground cinnamon

Chantilly cream
200ml (7fl oz) whipping cream
3 tbsp icing sugar
1 tbsp sherry

Put the prunes in a bowl and cover with Armagnac. Leave overnight to soak.

Preheat the oven to 150°C (300°F/Gas 2). Drain the prunes and reserve the soaking liquid for another use.

Beat the butter until soft and creamy, then add the almonds and icing sugar. Beat in the eggs, then add the flour and cinnamon and mix until incorporated. Put the mixture into the prepared flan case and arrange the prunes in a pretty pattern on top. Bake in the oven for about 50 minutes until firm to the touch and light brown on top.

Meanwhile, make the Chantilly cream. Simply whip the cream and sugar to soft peaks, then fold in the sherry. Serve immediately with the warm tart.

French Apple Tart

This is a classic French apple tart, and I make no apologies for including it, as everyone loves it. I use two types of apple – one quintessentially English – both for the flavours and for the ways in which they behave when cooked. The Cox's will "melt", while the Granny Smiths keep their shape. You could serve this with vanilla ice cream (see p.159), if you liked.

Serves 6

1 x 20cm (8in) Sweet Tart Pastry Case
  (pp.212–13)

Filling
4 large Cox's apples
60g (2oz) butter
75g (2½oz) sugar

4 tbsp Crème Pâtissière (p.214)
finely grated zest of 1 lemon

Topping
2 or 3 Granny Smith apples
juice of 1 lemon
4 tbsp apricot jam

Preheat the oven to 180°C (350°F/Gas 4) for baking the filling.

While the pastry case is cooling, peel and core the Cox's apples for the filling and chop finely. Put in a pan and cook gently in about 1 tbsp of water until completely soft. This should take about 20 minutes. Now add the butter and sugar and allow to cool (when the butter will solidify). This is now an apple purée.

Put the crème pâtissière on the bottom of the tart case, forming a very thin layer, followed by a layer of apple purée. Peel, core and finely slice the Granny Smith apples, putting them in a bowl with a little lemon juice as you go to prevent discolouring. Drain off any liquid and put the apple slices over the top of the filling in a spiral pattern.

Bake the tart in the oven for 30 minutes. Gently heat the apricot jam and push through a sieve. Carefully brush the sieved jam over the top of the tart, then allow to cool.

Pear Frangipane

I love the marzipan nuttiness of this frangipane cream, which goes so well with so many fruits. Try pears as here, or plums as below. You can have a plain frangipane cream by leaving out the cinnamon if you like. This makes quite a thin tart.

Makes
1 x 23cm
(9in) tart,
to serve 6

1 x 23cm (9in) Sweet Tart Pastry Case
  (pp.212–13)
3 ripe pears

Frangipane cream
75g (2½oz) unsalted butter
75g (2½oz) icing sugar
75g (2½oz) ground almonds
1 whole egg and 1 egg yolk, beaten
15g (½oz) plain flour
1 tsp ground cinnamon

Bake the tart case as described, then turn the oven to 150°C (300°F/Gas 2) ready to bake the pears and filling.

While the tart case is cooling, peel the pears. Cut them in half lengthways, core and put on a tray. Bake in the oven for 10 minutes, then allow them to rest while you prepare the almond cream.

To make the frangipane cream, cream together the butter and icing sugar until smooth, then add the ground almonds, eggs, flour and cinnamon. Spread the mixture over the bottom of the tart case. Arrange the baked pears in the cream in a neat pattern.

Bake in the oven for about 1 hour until the frangipane cream filling is firm. Allow to cool, and serve with cream.

TIP:

You can make a plum frangipane in exactly the same way. Halve and stone eight plums. Plums can be quite insipid, so many varieties (but not my favourite Victorias) might need a little sugar. Sprinkle the plums with 1 tsp caster sugar and put them on a tray, skin-side down. Sprinkle with another 1 tsp caster sugar. Bake the plums in the oven for 10 minutes as for the pears above and allow them to rest while you prepare the frangipane cream. Continue as described for the rest of the pear frangipane.

Rhubarb Bavarois

I love rhubarb, and it has such a short season that I take full advantage of it and use it in all sorts of dishes – ice cream, sauces, tarts, etc. It appears in the shops in early spring – usually forced young rhubarb, which is a wonderful pink colour. Here, I've used rhubarb in a bavarois, a dessert which is always custard-based, and topped it with a rhubarb jelly. Serve the bavarois and its jelly with a rhubarb compôte (see opposite), just to take full advantage of those wonderful flavours.

Serves 4

500g (1lb 2oz) forced young rhubarb, trimmed and cut into 3cm (1¼in) lengths
50g (1¾oz) caster sugar
2 gelatine leaves, softened in cold water
75ml (2½fl oz) milk
2 egg yolks
50ml (1½fl oz) double cream, whipped

Biscuit base
50g (1¾oz) ground almonds
50g (1¾oz) caster sugar, plus 2 tsp extra
1 egg

15g (½oz) unsalted butter, melted
10g (¼oz) plain flour
2 egg whites

Jelly
250ml (8fl oz) juice from cooking the rhubarb
4 gelatine leaves, softened in cold water

To serve
1 quantity Rhubarb Compôte (see opposite)

Line a baking tray of about 30 x 40cm (12 x 16in) with baking parchment.

First make the biscuit base. In a large bowl, combine all the ingredients except for the egg whites and the extra 2 tsp caster sugar. In a separate bowl, whisk the egg whites until soft peaks form, then add the extra caster sugar and whisk again. Use a little of the whisked egg white and sugar to slacken the almond mixture, then gently fold in the rest, so as not to lose too much air.

Spread the mixture on the prepared baking tray in a rough circle, slightly larger than 25cm (10in) in diameter, and bake in the oven for about 10 minutes (but check after 5) until it is a pale golden brown (it should have a sponge-type texture). Remove from the oven and leave to cool on the baking parchment.

Make the rhubarb purée for the bavarois. Put the rhubarb in a pan with the caster sugar and about 200ml (7fl oz) water. Cover and cook for 2–3 minutes until the rhubarb is tender, then strain the juice into a measuring jug (keep this for the jelly; you will need 250ml/8fl oz). Purée the fruit and push through a fine sieve.

To make the bavarois, heat the milk in a small saucepan and bring to the boil. Whisk the yolks with the remaining sugar. Pour the boiled milk over the egg mixture, whisking all the time. Pour into a clean pan over a low heat and stir until it starts to thicken and becomes a custard. Remove the custard from the heat and add the softened gelatine leaves. Stir until completely dissolved, then stir in the rhubarb purée. Allow to cool, then fold in the whipped cream.

Using six 5cm (2in) biscuit cutters, cut out six rings from the biscuit base, leaving the circle of biscuit in the bottom of each ring, then pour in the bavarois mixture. Leave to set in the refrigerator. This will take about 3 hours.

Meanwhile, make the jelly. Heat the reserved rhubarb juice, then melt the softened gelatine in it. Remove from the heat and allow to cool completely. When the bavarois custards have set, cover them with the cold liquid jelly and return to the refrigerator to set. This will take 20–30 minutes.

Take off the rings and place the little rhubarb creams onto serving plates. When you cut into them, you see the pretty contrast of pale biscuit, topped with pink cream, then the clear pink jelly.

Rhubarb Compôte

Rhubarb compôte, or roast rhubarb, goes very well with rhubarb bavarois. I like to emphasise a flavour such as rhubarb by complementing it with the same flavour, albeit in a slightly different form. So we might have a bavarois, which consists of a rhubarb custard topped with a rhubarb jelly, with a crowning touch of small pieces of rhubarb simply roasted and served with a sprinkling of sugar. Similarly, I could serve rhubarb tartlets with a rhubarb ice-cream.

Serves 4

3 rhubarb sticks, trimmed and cut into 2cm (¾in) lengths

2 tbsp caster sugar

Preheat the oven to 190°C (375°F/Gas 5). Put the rhubarb on a baking tray and bake in the oven for 20 minutes. Remove and allow to get cold before carefully lifting the pieces from the tray. Sprinkle with a little caster sugar before serving. Allow about three pieces of rhubarb per person.

TIP: *You can also make little rhubarb tartlets following the recipe (p.186), using a rhubarb purée or the roast rhubarb above with frangipane cream (p.177) or crème pâtissière (p.214). For this, hardly cook the rhubarb at all. For a rhubarb ice cream, cook 200g (7oz) forced young rhubarb with a little sugar and the juice of half an orange, then purée and add, when cool, to the vanilla ice cream recipe (p.159), but without the vanilla!*

Vanilla Panna Cotta with Concasse and Coulis of Exotic Fruit, with a Ginger Tuile

I love panna cotta and, although this is just a plain one, it becomes extra special when allied with exotic fruit. It's such a useful dessert, especially in the summer, when it would be just as delicious served simply with strawberries and cream.

Serves 4

2 gelatine leaves
400ml (14fl oz) double cream
75g (2½fl oz) caster sugar
seeds from 3 vanilla pods

Exotic fruit coulis
50g (1¾oz) caster sugar
250g (9oz) mixed diced fresh mango,
  papaya and peach

Exotic fruit salad
2 tbsp finely diced fresh mango
2 tbsp finely diced fresh papaya
2 tbsp finely diced green melon
½ peach, finely diced
2 strawberries, finely diced
juice of ½ lemon

To serve
deep-fried fresh mint leaves (p.29)
1 quantity Ginger Tuiles (p.202)

First, make the vanilla panna cotta. Soak the gelatine in cold water for 5 minutes. Put the cream, sugar and vanilla seeds in a small saucepan and bring slowly to the boil. Remove from the heat and leave to cool a little. Squeeze the excess water from the gelatine leaves and stir them into the cream mixture until melted. Pass the mixture through a fine sieve, and allow to cool until beginning to firm (this is to ensure the vanilla seeds do not go to the bottom of the moulds; they should be evenly dispersed). Pour the cream into four 100ml (3½fl oz) dariole moulds, and refrigerate for about 3 hours until set.

Meanwhile, make the coulis. Bring the sugar and 50ml (1¾fl oz) water to the boil in a small pan, stirring continuously. Reduce the heat slightly and simmer for 2 minutes, then remove the pan from the heat and leave to cool completely. Reserve 2 tbsp of the syrup for the fruit salad, and purée the remainder with the exotic fruit mix in a blender until smooth. Pass through a fine sieve and set aside.

When preparing the fruit salad, make sure that the fruit is nicely diced as described. Carefully toss the fruits in the reserved syrup and the lemon juice.

Turn the little moulds out onto individual serving plates. Arrange a little fruit salad beside them, and drizzle around the coulis. Garnish with the deep-fried mint leaves, and arrange a tuile at the side of each panna cotta.

Coconut Panna Cotta with Raspberry Coulis

I am a great coconut lover. When you are in a hurry, a panna cotta is one of the simplest puds you can prepare. It's very effective, and there are loads of things you can serve with it, such as an exotic fruit salad (p.180).

Serves 6–8

3 gelatine leaves
3 vanilla pods, split lengthways
300ml (10fl oz) double cream
240ml (8fl oz) coconut milk (from a tin)
100g (3½oz) caster sugar
2 tbsp crème fraîche

Raspberry coulis
250g (9oz) fresh raspberries
juice of 1 lemon
1 tbsp sugar syrup (p.168), or to taste

For the raspberry coulis, purée the fruit and lemon juice in a blender, pass through a fine sieve, then add the cold syrup. Set aside.

To make the panna cotta, immerse the gelatine leaves in plenty of cold water, leaving them to become floppy. Using a sharp knife, scrape out the seeds from the vanilla pods into a small saucepan. Add the cream, coconut milk and caster sugar, and bring to the boil. While the mixture is coming to the boil, squeeze the water from the gelatine leaves, then stir them into the boiling cream. Remove the pan from the heat. Strain the mixture through a fine sieve into a wide jug and allow it to cool, stirring occasionally so that you disperse the little specks of vanilla evenly throughout.

Once the mixture is cool enough for the vanilla seeds to remain suspended, whisk in the crème fraîche and pour the mixture into six to eight little moulds. Chill for at least 4 hours.

Turn the panna cottas out onto individual serving plates and serve surrounded by raspberry coulis.

Apple Cake with Calvados Ice Cream

This luscious cake is very much a pudding cake, so serve it with ice cream at the end of a meal, rather than for afternoon tea – although, really, there's no rule to say that you can't do that too, if you are feeling indulgent.

Serves 4

35g (1oz) butter, softened
75g (2½oz) caster sugar
1 egg
65g (2oz) plain flour
65g (2oz) self-raising flour
¼ tsp bicarbonate of soda
½ tsp cream of tartar
100ml (3½fl oz) milk

a few drops of vanilla extract
2½ Granny Smith apples
4 tbsp pine nuts
1 tbsp granulated sugar

To serve
1 quantity Calvados Ice Cream (p.159)

Preheat the oven to 170°C (325°F/Gas 3), and lightly grease a 20cm (8in) round cake tin with butter.

In a large bowl, cream together the butter and caster sugar until white and fluffy. Now add the egg and mix well. Fold in the flours, bicarbonate of soda and cream of tartar. Pour in the milk – you may need more to make it into a thick batter – and vanilla extract.

Peel and core the apples, then cut them into small cubes. Add them to the cake mixture.

Transfer the mixture to the prepared cake tin and sprinkle with the pine nuts and granulated sugar. Bake in the oven for 50 minutes.

Serve warm, cut into wedges, with some Calvados ice cream. (It can be served cold as well.)

Strawberry and Lemon Mille-feuille

This is obviously a summer version of mille-feuille, as it is in the summer that you will find the best strawberries and redcurrants. But you could also make this with pears in the autumn, and I once made a mille-feuille with caramelised plums. It may seem complicated, but the cream can be made well in advance, and kept in the refrigerator for a couple of days. It will make more than you need, but it is difficult to make in smaller quantities.

Serves 4

4 sheets filo pastry
50g (1¾oz) unsalted butter, melted
icing sugar, to dust

Lemon cream
finely grated zest and juice of 2 lemons
125g (4½oz) caster sugar
35g (1oz) butter

3 large eggs, plus 1 large egg yolk extra
150ml (5fl oz) double cream

To serve
200g (7oz) small strawberries, hulled
50g (1¾oz) icing sugar
200g (7oz) redcurrants, stalks removed
fresh mint leaves, to garnish

Preheat the oven to 200°C (400°F/Gas 6). Place your first sheet of filo on a lightly floured work surface, and brush with melted butter. Put another sheet on top. Cut into rectangles of about 12 x 6cm (5 x 2½in). Transfer to non-stick baking sheets or sheets lined with greaseproof paper. Do the same with the other two pieces of filo. You will need 12 rectangles in all. Brush melted butter across the tops of all the little rectangles and dust with lots of icing sugar. Put another baking sheet or some more greaseproof paper on top, which keeps the pastry flat, and bake in the oven for 5 minutes until golden.

To make the lemon cream, just bring the lemon juice and zest and the sugar to the boil. Mix in the butter until melted and smooth. Whisk the eggs and the extra egg yolk, then add the lemon liquid, whisking all the time. Pour into a clean pan, and gradually cook until smooth and thick. Leave to cool. All of this can be done in advance. When ready to serve, whip the cream until firm and fold it into half the lemon cream. (If you like it more lemony, just add a little more lemon cream.)

Cut about 50g (2oz) of the strawberries into small pieces, add the icing sugar and boil until thick. Remove from the heat and cool. Add the rest of the strawberries and the redcurrants.

To assemble, put a layer of pastry on the bottom, then some lemon cream. Using a slotted spoon, add a layer of strawberries and redcurrants. Repeat with another layer of filo, some cream and fruit, and finish with a layer of filo. Dust the tops of the mille-feuilles with icing sugar, and garnish with mint leaves.

Individual Wild Strawberry and Blueberry Tartlets

These look so pretty on the plate, and it's such a treat to enjoy the two fruits together when in their short season. We have loads of wild or alpine strawberries at Swinton and I use a lot of them. The only trouble is they take such a long time to pick!

Makes at least 8

Rich shortcrust pastry
170g (6oz) cold, unsalted butter
240g (8½oz) plain flour
2 tsp icing sugar
1 tbsp finely grated orange zest
pinch of salt
1 egg yolk
4 tbsp cold water

Filling and topping
½ quantity lemon cream (see Strawberry and Lemon Mille-feuille, p.184)
450g (1lb) wild strawberries and blueberries
icing sugar, to dust

To make the pastry, chop the butter roughly and put into a food processor with the flour. Process until the mixture looks like breadcrumbs, then add the icing sugar, orange zest and salt. Mix briefly. Add the egg yolk and water, and process until the mixture forms a ball. Remove, flatten slightly into a disc and wrap in cling film. Chill for 30 minutes.

Preheat the oven to 200°C (400°F/Gas 6). Lightly oil eight 8cm (3¼in) tartlet tins about 1.5cm (¾in) deep. Put a baking tray in the oven to heat through.

Remove the pastry from the refrigerator. Roll out thinly and use to line the tartlet tins. Prick the bottoms of the pastry cases with a fork, line with greaseproof paper and fill with beans or rice. Blind-bake on the hot baking tray for 12–15 minutes until golden. Remove from the oven and, if you think the pastry is not golden enough, remove the beans and put the pastry cases back in the oven for a further 5 minutes to dry them out. Allow to cool, then turn the tartlet cases out of the tins. (These can be made at least the day before.)

About an hour before serving, fill the tartlet cases with lemon cream, then arrange the strawberries and blueberries on top. Dust with icing sugar. Leave at room temperature.

Apple and Gooseberry Crumble with Calvados Ice Cream

Gooseberries have a very short season, and I absolutely adore them. I love their sharpness, and tend to put them with something like apple, which can temper that acidity. I couldn't have a book without a gooseberry recipe in it – and I could have given you gooseberry fool, bavarois, mousse... When something is in season, you really must enjoy it.

Serves 4

Crumble
110g (3¾oz) very cold butter, cut into cubes
80g (2¾oz) plain flour
50g (1¾oz) porridge oats
30g (1oz) shelled hazelnuts, skinned
80g (3oz) soft brown sugar

Filling
600g (1¼lb) cooking apples or Cox's apples
40g (1½oz) unsalted butter, melted

300g (10½oz) gooseberries, topped and tailed
80g (3oz) caster sugar, or to taste
juice of 1 lemon

To serve
1 quantity Calvados Ice Cream (p.159)

Preheat the oven to 180°C (350°F/Gas 4). Grease four individual pie dishes well with unsalted butter.

First, make the crumble. Put the very cold diced butter and the flour in a food processor. Process until the mixture looks like fine breadcrumbs. Add the hazelnuts and brown sugar and pulse for 5 seconds, now add the porridge oats and pulse again for 2 seconds. Set aside in a bowl until needed.

To prepare the filling, peel, core and slice the apples, and put the slices in a large saucepan with the lemon juice. Cook with 25g (¾oz) of the butter over a low heat just until tender, about 10 minutes. Now add the gooseberries and cook for a further 2 minutes. Add the caster sugar, and taste for sweetness. Fold in the remaining melted butter.

Divide the filling between the prepared individual pie dishes. Sprinkle the crumble mixture evenly all over the surface. Bake in the oven for 25 minutes until it forms a golden crust. It may need a little longer.

Serve hot with a scoop of Calvados ice cream on each serving.

Bread and Biscuits

Home-made breads and biscuits are delicious, much better than store-bought versions. If you have time to make them, it's really worthwhile, and your guests will be truly appreciative of the results.

Baking bread does not play much part in my television school for cooks, but it does in my cookery courses in Yorkshire. Bread is the staff of life, after all. I think baking bread is one of the basic skills that we should all possess. I would even go so far as to say that children should learn how to bake bread as early as possible: it's a good play activity for them – kneading the dough and shaping it – but it would also introduce them to the satisfaction of making something to eat by and for themselves, and initiate them into the world of good home-made flavours.

It is quite costly to buy good bread these days, and it is also hard to find something really tasty that doesn't stick to the roof of your mouth. That's why you should try to make your own. And think how wonderful your kitchen and home will smell – estate agents apparently recommend baking bread before prospective buyers come to view! The recipes here are fairly easy and straightforward, and display a variety of influences from around Europe. I have a classic French bread, a brioche-like plait, an Italian focaccia and olive oil bread rolls, a north European rye bread and an Irish soda bread. Most are served plain, but a few have ideas for different flavourings or toppings. All, apart from the soda bread, involve fresh yeast. This is increasingly available, but, if you can't get hold of it, use dried yeast, following the instructions on the packet (a rough guideline is half the quantity of dried as is specified for fresh).

Bread may take time to make – involving kneading, resting, proving, rising, and baking – but meanwhile you can be doing other things, leaving the bread to get on by itself. You can make bread well in advance, too, as it freezes well. Just remember to allow enough time for it to defrost.

Baking biscuits is almost as satisfactory as baking bread. The biscuits here aren't the sort you would have for morning coffee or afternoon tea (well, I suppose you could fill the brandy snaps with cream for tea). They are here because I use them as a decoration and accompaniment for desserts. A creamy dessert or ice cream is incredibly enhanced by the look, taste, and texture of a crisp biscuit. Tuiles are French biscuits, and they are very versatile. They can be made in different sizes and shapes, and there is a number of flavourings that you can add to ring the changes. The Italians are good at biscuits, too, and there are a couple of delicious Italian recipes here. I have included a pancake recipe which, although it is used only in the book in a savoury main course, could be made for serving at tea-time or as a dessert, perhaps with icing sugar or honey, and some lemon juice. But I do like my pancakes thin.

Focaccia

This Italian bread is gorgeous. You can bake it plain, or top it with a variety of ingredients: coarse sea salt, sliced lemon, crushed garlic, chopped fresh rosemary, mint or coriander, sliced red onion or ground cumin.

**Makes
2 loaves**

500g (1lb 2oz) strong white plain flour
20g (¾oz) fresh yeast
300ml (10fl oz) water, at room temperature

10g (¼oz) salt
350ml (12fl oz) extra virgin olive oil

Put the flour in a large bowl, make a well in the centre, and add the yeast, crumbling it up as you do so. Now add the water and mix together to form a dough. Transfer to a floured work surface, and tear and knead the dough for about 10 minutes until it is soft and elastic. Add the salt now. Continue tearing and kneading for 5 more minutes.

Divide the dough into two balls. Put about 1 tbsp oil into each of the two bowls, and put the dough balls in. Roll around, then cover with cling film and leave to rise until doubled in volume; about 1–1½ hours (depending on the temperature of the room).

Put about 3 tbsp oil in each of two 18-cm (7-in) round tins. After the dough has risen, knock it down and flatten it. Stretch each piece into a circle to fit its oiled tin. Put each circle of dough in a tin and, using your fingertips, press dents and holes in the dough, so that the oil underneath comes popping through.

Now add the chosen topping, pressing it into the dough to help the flavours penetrate. Or simply sprinkle some coarse sea salt over the top. Cover loosely and leave for another 30 minutes to rise.

Preheat the oven to 220°C (425°F/Gas 7).

Bake the focaccia in the oven for 15–20 minutes until golden. Turn the oven down to 150°C (300°F/Gas 2) and bake for a further 10 minutes. Remove from the tins, and cool on a wire rack.

French Bread

This is a classic French bread recipe, but you can also add some flavourings if you like. If you want these *inside* the bread, add them at the beginning (saffron, bacon, sun-dried tomatoes, black olives). If you want them to go on the *outside* of the bread, sprinkle on after the second proving (sesame, poppy, or sunflower seeds, stoned olives, bacon and onion bits, sun-dried tomato – anything you fancy, really). You can also make rolls from this recipe: these should be 45–50g (1½–1¾oz) each, and will take 10–15 minutes to bake at the temperature below.

Makes	500g (1lb 2 oz) strong white plain flour	350ml (12fl oz) water, at room temperature
4 baguettes	15g (½oz) fresh yeast, crumbled	10g (¼oz) salt

Mix the flour and yeast in a large bowl, make a well in the centre of the mixture, and add the water. Mix until the dough comes together, then knead and stretch on a lightly floured work surface for 10 minutes until the dough is elastic. Next, add the salt, and knead and stretch for a further 5 minutes. Transfer the dough to a floured bowl, and leave to rise until doubled in volume, which will take about 1 hour.

When the dough has doubled in volume, knock back, then roll it out on a floured baking tray into four sticks, or baguettes, and leave to rise again, making sure you have left enough space between each to allow for spreading. This will take a good 30 minutes.

Preheat the oven to 220°C (425°F/Gas 7).

Bake the baguettes in the oven for about 10 minutes. Reduce the oven temperature to 180°C (350°/Gas 4), and bake for a further 15 minutes. Cool on a wire rack.

TIP: *Cut French bread – preferably home-made – into slices for croûtons, and put in a preheated 150°C (300°F/Gas 2) oven for 20 minutes until dried out.*

Rich Bread Plait

This is a rich bread, almost a substitute brioche, and it keeps well (anything with fat in it keeps well). It has a great taste, and it makes unbelievable toast, as well as Melba toast. Use it as the base of canapés or, toasted, as an accompaniment to pâtés.

Makes 1 loaf

500g (1lb 2oz) strong white plain flour
15g (½oz) fresh yeast, crumbled
75g (2½oz) butter
300ml (10fl oz) milk

1 tsp caster sugar
1 egg, beaten
10g (¼oz) salt
1 egg yolk, mixed with 1 tbsp water, to glaze

Mix the flour with the yeast in a large bowl. Gently heat the butter in a pan with the milk and sugar until the butter has melted. Allow to cool slightly (to blood heat), then beat in the egg. Stir this mixture into the flour, form into a soft dough, and knead on a lightly floured work surface for 10 minutes. Add the salt, and continue kneading and stretching for another 5 minutes. Put the dough in a floured bowl, cover, and leave to rise for about 1 hour until doubled in volume.

Take the dough, and knock it back. Roll into a thin sausage, and cut into three equal widths lengthways, keeping attached at the end furthest from you. Plait the three strands together, then seal the end nearest to you. Put the plait on a floured tray, cover loosely, and leave to rise for about another hour until doubled in size.

Preheat the oven to 200°C (400°F/Gas 6).

Brush the plait with the egg and water glaze, and bake in the oven for 30 minutes until the bread sounds hollow when tapped on the bottom. Cool on a wire rack.

Black Olive Bread Rolls

You can use this recipe to make a plain olive bread, just with olive oil (you might like to add some fresh herbs), and you can also substitute green olives for the black, if you wish. I like making this dough into rolls: you can cut these into whatever shape you like, but square is the easiest.

Makes
20–25 rolls

500g (1lb 2oz) strong plain white flour
15g (½oz) fresh yeast, crumbled
350ml (12fl oz) water, at room temperature

40ml (1½fl oz) olive oil
15g (½oz) salt
about 2 rounded tbsp chopped black olives

First, mix the flour and yeast in a large bowl, and make a well in the centre. Add the water, and mix until it begins to come together into a dough. Next, add the oil to bring it together completely, then add the salt. Knead for at least 15 minutes. Knead in the black olives at the last minute.

Roll out the dough until it is about 2cm (¾in) thick, and put on a floured cloth in a gratin dish about 22cm (9in) square. Cover loosely, and leave the dough to rise for about 1½ hours until it has doubled in volume.

Preheat the oven to 220°C (425°F/Gas 7).

When the dough has risen, turn it out carefully onto a floured board and, using a floured knife, cut into squares of about 4cm (1¾in). Carefully transfer the squares of dough to a baking tray, cover, and leave to rise for about 15 minutes more.

Bake the rolls in the oven for about 12 minutes until golden. Cool on a wire rack.

Rye Bread

This is an unusual bread, but a deeply delicious one, good served with many of the soups and starters in this book. It toasts well, and I particularly like it with cheese. It's a light rye bread and doesn't keep for long. It should be eaten within 24 hours.

Makes 3 baguettes

300g (10oz) plain flour
150g (5¼oz) rye flour
15g (½oz) fresh yeast, crumbled

400ml (14fl oz) water, at room temperature
1 tbsp hazelnut oil
10g (¼oz) salt

Mix together the flours and yeast in a large bowl, and make a well in the centre. Mix in the water and oil until it forms a dough. Knead for about 10 minutes on a lightly floured work surface, then add the salt and knead again for about 5 minutes. Put the dough in a floured bowl, cover loosely, and leave to rise for about 1 hour until doubled in volume.

After the dough has risen, split it into three pieces. Shape into baguettes, and leave to rise on a baking sheet for about 45 minutes (but check after 30 minutes) until the dough has again doubled in volume.

Preheat the oven to 220°C (425°F/Gas 7).

Transfer the baking tray to the oven, and bake the baguettes for 15 minutes. Reduce the oven temperature to 150°C (300°F/Gas 2), and bake for another 15 minutes, checking to see how the bread is doing. Turn the baguettes upside down, and pop back in the oven for another 5 minutes (just to be sure). Cool on a wire rack.

Soda Bread

This soda bread would go well with all the soups in the book. It's great for breakfast, too, particularly as it's so quick and easy to make. This is because it contains no yeast, and therefore does not require any proving time before baking.

Makes 1 loaf

500g (1lb 2oz) plain flour
1 tsp salt
1 rounded tsp bicarbonate of soda

about 500ml (16fl oz) buttermilk or soured milk (see tip below)
2 tbsp sunflower oil

Preheat the oven to 220°C (425°F/Gas 7). Put all the dry ingredients in a bowl, and make a well in the centre. Pour in the buttermilk or soured milk and the oil, and lightly bring together to form a soft but not sticky dough.

Knead minimally on a lightly floured work surface. Put on a floured tray. Make a cross in the middle of the top of the dough, and bung into the oven for 20 minutes. Reduce the oven temperature to 150°C (300°F/Gas 2), and bake for a further 25 minutes until dark golden in colour. Cool on a wire rack.

TIP:

To make soured milk – which could replace the buttermilk in the recipe above – add 2 tsp white wine vinegar to 500ml (16fl oz) full-fat milk, and leave overnight.

Pancakes

I don't have a dessert pancake recipe in the book: these pancakes are used in the Venison en Croûte (p.112). They are good, though, by themselves. If you wanted them a little sweeter, simply add about 60g (2oz) of caster sugar to the batter. They are useful as you can keep them for a day or so until needed, and they freeze very well.

Makes 6 pancakes

120g (4½oz) plain flour
1 egg
25g (scant 1oz) butter, melted

300ml (10fl oz) full-fat milk
olive oil

Mix the flour, egg, melted butter, and milk together, then beat the mixture well until you have a smooth batter.

Heat a little olive oil in a large 20cm (8in) non-stick frying pan or crêpe pan, and ladle in enough mixture to cover the bottom. Cook for a moment or two on each side. Remove carefully from the pan, and put to one side, between two sheets of baking parchment.

Make the remaining five pancakes, and stack on top of the first, using more baking parchment in layers in between to prevent the pancakes sticking together.

Biscotti di Prato

Years ago, I attended a cookery school in a palazzo called Cappezzano in Italy. I had a wonderful time, and learned so much, including this recipe. These biscotti are perfect for dipping into Vin Santo, but they also work well as a final touch to desserts.

Makes 6 pancakes

250g (oz) plain flour
150g (5½oz) caster sugar
1 egg, plus 1 extra egg yolk, beaten
1 tsp baking powder

pinch of salt
50g (1¾oz) butter, melted
50g (1¾oz) whole almonds
1 tsp finely grated orange zest

Preheat the oven to 180°C (350°F/Gas 4). Grease and flour two baking sheets at least 37cm (15cm) long.

Pour the flour into a mound on a work surface. Put the sugar, one egg, baking powder, and salt in a well in the centre. Add the melted butter, and gradually work the flour into the other ingredients. Mix with your hands until smooth. Knead in the almonds and orange zest thoroughly, then keep kneading for about 5 minutes, sprinkling with extra flour if needed. Don't work too much, though!

Divide the dough in half. On a floured work surface, roll each piece of dough into a log 5–6cm (2–2½in) wide. Set the logs at least 5cm (2in) apart on the baking sheet. Brush with the extra beaten egg yolk to glaze.

Bake in the oven for 15 minutes, then reduce the temperature to 170°C (325°F/Gas 3), and cook for a further 20 minutes. Remove from the oven, and cut the logs into diagonal slices 1cm (½in) thick. Lay the slices back on the baking sheets, and return to the oven for another 5 minutes. Allow to cool on wire racks.

Sicilian Creams

Another Italian speciality, Sicilian creams are very sweet, quite soft, and hollow, so they can be filled. They are lovely with many desserts and, filled with crème pâtissière (p.214), flavoured or unflavoured, they make a tempting treat on their own.

Makes about
12 biscuits

200g (7oz) self-raising flour
60g (2oz) butter
110g (4oz) caster sugar
1 tsp finely grated lemon zest
1 tsp vanilla extract

1 egg yolk, plus 1 extra, beaten, to glaze
4 tbsp milk
1 tbsp Amaretto or Grand Marnier liqueur
whipped double cream, to serve
icing sugar, to dust

Preheat the oven to 180°C (350°F/Gas 4). Lightly grease a baking tray. Sift the flour into a bowl, and rub in the butter. Add the sugar and mix. Combine the lemon zest, vanilla extract, one egg yolk, and milk. Pour into a well in the centre of the flour mixture with the liqueur. Mix into a pliable dough, adding a little water if necessary. Knead on a lightly floured work surface until smooth. Wrap in cling film, and chill for about 20 minutes.

Roll out the dough to 1cm (½in) thick, and cut into 5cm (2in) rounds with a biscuit cutter. (You can re-roll the mixture.) Put the rounds on the baking tray, and brush with a little of the beaten egg yolk. Bake for 15–20 minutes until light golden brown. Leave to cool for a minute, then split each one in half and sandwich with the cream. Dust with icing sugar.

Brandy Snap Biscuits

Brandy snaps are a useful garnish in your repertoire. As they come out of the oven, they can be shaped into tubes – great served with ice cream or mousses – or they can be made into little baskets – wonderful to serve ice cream or chopped fruit in.

Makes
plenty for 8

50g (1¾oz) unsalted butter, softened
50g (1¾oz) caster sugar

50g (1¾oz) golden syrup
30g (1oz) plain flour

Whisk the butter in a bowl until pale. Add the caster sugar and whisk again. Now put the golden syrup in a pan, and heat until it is just runny. Add the golden syrup to the butter mixture and whisk again, before adding the flour and mixing well. Put in a small bowl and chill for 3 hours.

Preheat the oven to 180°C (350°F/Gas 4). Form teaspoons of the mixture into balls, and put on a baking mat or greased baking sheet. Cook three at a time, as they spread. Bake for about 10 minutes. Remove from the oven, and leave for 30 seconds. Lift off the tray with a palette knife. To shape them, work speedily, as they harden very quickly. To make baskets, drape over the buttered outside of dariole moulds or ramekins. For tubes, wrap around a knife sharpener or something similar. As the biscuits cool, they will solidify in their shape.

Tuiles

Tuiles are crisp little French biscuits – named after tiles! – which are wonderful to serve with soft desserts. You can cook the biscuit mixture in one large piece and break pieces off; you can shape the mixture in a template; or you can cook it in spoonfuls, which will spread to a circle and can then be served like that or shaped – into tubes or baskets (see Brandy Snap Biscuits, p.201, for how to do this). This is the basic recipe for tuiles, which can be flavoured (see below). But, I do warn you, these are very difficult to get right. It's probably the trickiest recipe in the book!

Makes plenty to serve 8

75g (2½oz) unsalted butter, softened
75g (2½oz) icing sugar, sifted
1 egg whites

1 egg
75g (2½oz) plain flour

Whisk the butter until pale, then slowly add the sifted icing sugar, whisking all the time until incorporated. Now add the egg whites very slowly, bit by bit, making sure they are well mixed in before you add the next bit. Next, add the whole egg. Finally, sift in the flour (and chosen flavouring, if using), mixing well. Transfer to a small bowl, cover, and chill for a couple of hours.

Preheat the oven to 170°C (325°F/Gas 3). Line a baking tray with non-stick baking parchment. Spread the mixture over the entire tray to make a one-piece tuiles that is to be broken up, or to make individual tuiles drop dessertspoons or teaspoons of mixture on the tray at intervals (only two or three at a time). Alternatively, you could cut out a suitable shape in a flat, plastic template, and set the template on the lined tray. Spread a thin layer of mixture into the shape of the template, and carefully remove the template.

Transfer the baking tray to the oven, and bake the tuiles for 8–10 minutes until golden and just beginning to brown around the edges. Very quickly lift the tuile or tuiles off the baking sheet using a palette knife, and twist to make a shape if required. This biscuit goes hard straight away, so you need to work quickly. Eat that day.

Ginger or cinnamon tuiles Add 2 tsp ground ginger or cinnamon.
Coffee tuiles Add 3 tsp very finely ground coffee.
Poppy seed tuiles Add 1 tbsp poppy seeds.

Basics

Chicken Stock

The most useful stock of them all, chicken stock can be made with the bones of one chicken or of many, depending on circumstances. If you'd like the stock to look darker, roast the bones in a hot oven for an hour before you start. Any other poultry stock, including duck and turkey, can be made in a similar way.

Makes
about 1 litre
(1³/₄ pints)

450g (1lb) raw chicken bones
olive oil
½ bottle white wine
1 onion, roughly chopped
1 carrot, roughly chopped

1 celery stick, roughly chopped
2 sprigs of flat-leaf parsley
2 sprigs of thyme
2 bay leaves
1 tsp black peppercorns

Chop the bones into small pieces, then brown on all sides in hot oil in a large pan. Add the wine, and simmer for 5 minutes until the liquid has reduced to a couple of tablespoons. Add the vegetables, flavourings, and enough cold water to cover. Simmer for about 1 hour. Skim occasionally, but do not stir, as you want to create a clear chicken stock. Strain through a fine sieve, and allow to cool. Discard the solids, and remove all the fat from the stock's surface. Refrigerate if not using immediately, for no more than three days.

Game Stock

This is good for any game dishes, soups or sauces, and you can use the carcasses or bones of any game creatures – pheasants, partridges, venison, rabbit, etc. When game is in season in the autumn, make lots of game stock and freeze it.

Makes
about 1 litre
(1³/₄ pints)

2kg (4½lb) game bones
1 pig's trotter (optional)
2 large onions, quartered
olive oil
2 tbsp tomato purée
1 bottle red wine
2 carrots, chopped

75g (2½oz) mushrooms, chopped
3 tomatoes, quartered
1 celery stick, chopped
6 garlic cloves, chopped
handful of thyme
6 bay leaves
2 tsp black peppercorns

Preheat the oven to 220°C (425°F/Gas 7). Chop the game bones and pig's trotters into small chunks. Put in a roasting pan with half the onions and a sprinkling of oil, and cook until dark brown (30–40 minutes), turning once. When cooked, drain off all the fat.

Put the bones in a large saucepan along with the onion, add the tomato purée and red wine, and cook for 1 minute. Now add the remaining vegetables and other ingredients, and stir well. Add enough cold water to cover the bones, bring to the boil, and simmer for about 2–3 hours. Do not stir, keep skimming as the impurities come to the surface. Strain the stock through a fine sieve, put back in a clean pan, and reduce again for 1 hour. Allow to cool. This keeps in the refrigerator for about five days, or you can freeze it.

Meat Stock or Brown Stock

Ask your butcher to let you have some bones for this: it is particularly useful if the bones contain marrow. Use it for all beef and lamb dishes. You might notice that I don't season my stocks: that is because I season the sauce or dish later.

Makes about 1 litre (1³/₄ pints)

2kg (4½lb) beef or veal bones
2 large onions, quartered
2 carrots, roughly chopped
2 celery sticks, roughly chopped
2 bay leaves

2 sprigs of thyme
2 tsp black peppercorns
4 cloves
2 sprigs of parsley

Preheat the oven to 220°C (425°F/Gas 7). Roast the bones with one of the onions in the oven for about an hour. This length of time gives a good colour and flavour to the stock.

Transfer the bones and onion to a large saucepan. Add the remaining ingredients, and cover everything with cold water. Bring to the boil, reduce the heat slightly, and simmer for about 3–4 hours, topping it up with water when necessary and skimming occasionally. Strain through a fine sieve, discard the solids, and allow the stock to cool. Store in the refrigerator, and skim off and discard the fat before using the stock. It keeps, covered, in a refrigerator for up to five days, or it can be frozen.

Veal Jus

Veal jus is fantastic in sauces, and is made in virtually the same way as the meat stock above, simply with the addition of a pig's trotter, a few mushrooms, and some major or minor reduction. It keeps very well.

Makes about 500ml (16fl oz)

3kg (6½lb) veal bones
1 pig's trotter, split in half
2 large onions, quartered
2 carrots, roughly chopped
2 celery sticks, roughly chopped
100g (3½oz) mushrooms, finely sliced

2 bay leaves
2 sprigs of thyme
2 tsp black peppercorns
4 cloves
2 sprigs of parsley

Follow the instructions for the meat stock above, roasting the bones and trotter with one of the onions, then simmering everything together for 4 hours. Strain through a fine sieve, discard the solids, and reduce the stock by about half.

To make the jus into an even stronger sauce, a demi-glace, bring it up to a simmer once more, and reduce it by about half again, when it will have a richer, more intense flavour. (When it gets to this consistency, you need to use less of it.) Allow to cool. Keep in the refrigerator, and discard any fat that forms on the surface. The stock keeps, covered, in the refrigerator for up to seven days – or, of course, you can freeze it.

Fish Stock

The important thing about making stock from fish bones, as opposed to meat or poultry bones, is that it mustn't be cooked too long; if it is, it becomes cloudy. And you must always use white fish bones, not oily salmon or trout bones.

Makes
about 700ml
(1¼ pints)

2kg (4½lb) cleaned bones, skins, head, tails, and fins of white fish
½ bulb fennel, roughly chopped
1 leek, roughly chopped
1 onion, roughly chopped
6 sprigs of flat-leaf parsley
2 tsp white peppercorns
2 bay leaves
½ bottle white wine

Rinse the fish bones and trimmings of any blood, and make sure that any organs have been removed. Put all of the ingredients in a large pan, and cover with cold water. Bring slowly to the boil, then reduce the heat slightly and simmer for 30 minutes, skimming off any impurities occasionally.

Strain through a fine sieve, discard the solids, and leave the stock to cool before refrigerating (unless using straight away). The stock keeps, covered, in the refrigerator for a couple of days only; alternatively, once it has cooled, it can be frozen.

Vegetable Stock

Suitable for vegetarian recipes, this aromatic stock is sometimes known as a "court-bouillon" or "nage". It is traditionally used to poach fish and shellfish, and in certain sauces. It can also be used in some chicken and veal recipes.

Makes about
1.75–2 litres
(3–3½ pints)

2 onions, roughly chopped
2 leeks, roughly chopped
2 carrots, roughly chopped
2 celery sticks, roughly chopped
2 bay leaves
2 garlic cloves
2 stalks lemongrass
2 sprigs of tarragon
2 sprigs of flat-leaf parsley
2 tsp black peppercorns
½ bottle white wine

Put the vegetables and all the flavourings in a large pan with the wine, and bring to the boil. Reduce the heat slightly, and allow to simmer for 5 minutes before adding 1.5 litres (2¾ pints) water and bringing back to the boil. Reduce the heat, and simmer the stock for a further 30 minutes, skimming occasionally.

Leave to cool before straining through a fine sieve and discarding the solids. This stock keeps for only a couple of days in the refrigerator, after this the flavours deteriorate.

Puff Pastry

I recommend that you make the quantity given in the recipe, not less. If you have any pastry left over, save it wrapped, in its layers, in the refrigerator or freezer. The pastry is made in two stages, which I have called "first ball" and "second ball".

Makes a
good 1kg
(2¹/₄lb)

First ball
500g (1lb 2oz) plain flour
10g (¼oz) salt
80g (3oz) unsalted butter, melted

Second ball
250g (9oz) plain flour
500g (1lb 2oz) butter, cubed

For the first ball, mix the flour and salt in a large bowl, then make a well in the centre. Add the melted butter and about 175ml (6fl oz) water, and mix to make a smooth dough, adding more water – up to 30ml (1fl oz) – if necessary. Shape the dough into a ball, and cut a deep cross into the surface. Cover with cling film, and chill for 30 minutes.

For the second ball, blend the butter with the flour, and form the mixture into a ball. Wrap in cling film and chill also.

Put the first ball on a floured work surface. Pull it from the middle into the shape of a four-leaved clover, making a space in the centre. Unwrap the second ball, and place it in the centre. Fold the "clover leaves" over the top to enclose. Using a rolling pin, roll the dough into a rectangular shape about 46cm (18in) long and 15cm (6in) wide. Fold each end inwards to form a three-layered square. Place on a floured tray, cover, and return to the refrigerator for a further 30 minutes.

Repeat the rolling and folding process twice more, again refrigerating in between. Finally, return the pastry to the refrigerator for at least 2 hours before using.

Hot-Water Suet Crust Pastry

Suet puddings are usually made with cold suet pastry, but I prefer to use a hot pastry: the hot water melts the suet, so the pastry is smoother. Don't make it too thick, and you must knead it after mixing until it is lovely and smooth.

Makes
about 600g
(1lb 5oz)

400g (14oz) plain flour
175g (6oz) beef suet
½ tsp baking powder

2 tsp salt
180ml (6fl oz) boiling water

Simply put all the dry ingredients in a bowl. Make a well in the centre, and mix in the boiling water. Knead the dough until smooth then, working swiftly, roll and shape as the recipe requires.

Choux Pastry

I love choux pastry – both making it and eating it. It's so light and tasty, it is almost a comfort food for me. It is incredibly versatile, too, as it is not only used for making choux buns, profiteroles (p.158), and éclairs, but can also be added to mashed potatoes, to make pommes dauphines; to a fish purée for quenelles; and to a myriad of other savoury, usually deep-fried or baked, dishes.

Serves 4

100g (3½oz) unsalted butter
140g (5oz) plain flour

3 eggs

Bring 250ml (8fl oz) water and the butter to the boil together in a medium pan, remove from the heat, and add the flour all at the same time. Mix well with a wooden spoon to make a thick roux – it should come away from the sides of the pan. Put the pan back on the heat if the roux needs drying out a little more.

Allow the roux to cool for 15 minutes, then beat in the eggs one by one. The choux should hold its shape when piped, which is why you add the eggs gradually.

Use as required, but swiftly, in the individual recipes.

Sweet Tart Pastry Case

This sweet pastry can be used to make the tarts on pp.160, 162, 164, 174, 175 and 177, and it's a useful thing to have around for a quick pudding. I prefer to use a flan ring on a baking sheet to an enclosed tart tin – the pastry case is not so likely to break when you remove it from the ring. You could make this pastry without the sugar if you wanted a good pastry for savoury tarts.

Makes
1 x 20–23cm
(8–9in) tart,
to serve 6

150g (5½oz) plain flour
80g (3oz) cold unsalted butter
30g (1oz) icing sugar

1 large egg yolk
3 tbsp cold water

Put the flour in a food processor, and add the cold butter. Mix until it resembles breadcrumbs, then add the icing sugar. Pulse, then add the egg yolk and water.

Alternatively, to make by hand, put the flour in a bowl, and add the cold butter in cubes. Mix together with your fingertips until the texture is like breadcrumbs. Add the icing sugar, and make a well in the middle. Put in the egg yolk and water, and mix together to form a soft dough.

Put the mixture on a lightly floured work surface. Bring the dough together into a smooth pastry, being careful not to overwork it. Form into a slightly flattened disc, wrap in cling film, and chill for about 20 minutes.

Roll out the pastry on a floured work surface to about 3mm (⅛in) thick, then use to line a buttered tart tin, or flan ring on a baking sheet, of 20–23cm (8–9in) diameter and 2.5cm (1in) deep. Make sure that you get the pastry even all around. Keep the trimmings (for lattices or decorations). Prick the base of the pastry with a fork, and put the tin in the refrigerator to allow the pastry to rest and chill for as long as possible, or at least 20 minutes.

Preheat the oven to 200°C (400°F/Gas 6). Line the pastry case with greaseproof paper, and pour in baking beans, rice, or dried beans. Bake blind for 15 minutes. Remove the beans and paper, then return the pastry case to the oven for a further 3–5 minutes. At this point, if you liked – and it does make the case a little stronger – you could brush the bottom and sides with egg white, before returning the pastry case to the oven.

Crème Pâtissière

This is what is sometimes called "confectioner's custard" or "pastry cream". It is served cold, used as a base or filling for tarts, flans and profiteroles. My students often think they have gone wrong because it is so thick – but it's meant to be like that!

Makes about 400ml

4 egg yolks
100g (3½oz) caster sugar
3 tsp cornflour

30g (1oz) plain flour
350ml (12fl oz) full-fat milk

Whisk the egg yolks and sugar together until pale and creamy, then add the cornflour and flour. Put the milk in a small, heavy saucepan and bring to the boil. Now whisk the scalded milk slowly into the egg mixture. Pour the mixture into a clean pan, and bring slowly to the boil, really beating to remove any lumps. Allow to simmer for 1 minute until it thickens. Put through a fine sieve into a bowl, and allow to cool. Cover with cling film, ensuring that the cling film touches the crème pâtissière, to prevent a skin forming. Allow to cool completely before using.

Crème Anglaise

This versatile crème anglaise can be both a warm sauce to accompany desserts and the base of my ice cream. Both can be flavoured in different ways. For using in ice creams, see the vanilla ice cream on p.159.

4 large egg yolks
50g (1¾oz) caster sugar

250ml (8fl oz) full-fat milk
1 vanilla pod, split lengthways

In a bowl, whisk the egg yolks and sugar together until pale. In a heavy saucepan, boil the milk with the seeds from the vanilla pod and the pod itself. Remove and discard the vanilla pod. Pour the milk into the egg mixture, whisking all the time, then put back in a clean pan and bring the heat up slowly. Using a wooden spoon, stir until the mixture starts to thicken, then quickly remove from the heat. Be careful not to overheat, otherwise it will become scrambled egg. To test whether the crème anglaise is cooked, draw a line along the back of the wooden spoon with your finger; if the crème anglaise remains still, without filling in the line immediately, it is ready.

Now add the flavouring spirit (if using). Finally, pass the crème anglaise through a fine sieve into a bowl, and cover with cling film. This should touch the surface of the crème anglaise, to prevent a skin forming. Transfer to the refrigerator until cold.

Coffee Crème Anglaise Add 2 tsp fresh finely ground coffee.
Poire Williams Crème Anglaise Add 2 tbsp liqueur.
Calvados (or brandy, or rum) Crème Anglaise Add spirit to taste (about 2 tbsp).

Ravioli

If making ravioli to go in a consommé (as on p.18), I would add more egg yolks, and no white, because the egginess is what you require. The more yolks you use, the quicker pasta dries out, so always cover well. You can add flavourings, such as saffron by boiling this in the water for the pasta.

Serves 4

200g "00" Italian plain flour, plus extra
   for dusting
3 medium egg yolks
1 whole medium egg

1 tbsp olive oil
1 tbsp water
salt

To make the pasta, process the flour, egg yolks, egg, olive oil, water and salt together in a processor to form rough crumbs. Tip out onto a floured surface, form into a ball and knead lightly for a few minutes until smooth. Cover with cling film and rest in the refrigerator for 1 hour.

Cut the ravioli dough into four and keep it covered when it is standing (to stop it drying out). Take one of the pieces and start putting through the largest setting of the pasta machine. Keep reducing the aperture until you get the right thickness (normally the thinnest setting). Make sure to use enough flour otherwise it will stick.

Lay strips of the pasta over a ravioli tin, carefully pressing it into each hole. Spoon a little of the chosen filling into each hole, and then lay another sheet of pasta on top. Run a rolling pin over the ravioli to seal. Finally cut into individual ravioli and pop them out of the tin. Place on a floured tray, cover and refrigerate until ready to cook. Repeat until all of the dough and filling are used up.

If you haven't got a ravioli tin, take a ribbon of pasta, and lay on a floured surface. Put a ½-walnut-size ball of your chosen filling on to it, at intervals, leaving a 3cm gap between each one. Glaze with egg all round and lay another ribbon of pasta on top. Seal well, then cut out the ravioli, making sure you get all the air out of each piece. Put onto a floured tray and refrigerate until ready to cook.

Vinaigrette

This is a great everyday vinaigrette, one which is extremely handy to have in your larder ready for a lunch-time salad. Don't store it in the refrigerator, though, as this makes it cloudy and masks the vinaigrette's tang.

Makes 300ml
(10fl oz)

1 garlic clove, peeled but not chopped
30ml (1fl oz) white wine vinegar
2 tsp Dijon mustard
150ml (5fl oz) olive oil

150ml (5fl oz) sunflower oil
1 tsp caster sugar
salt and pepper

Put the garlic in a screw-top jar with a tight-fitting lid. In a bowl, mix the vinegar and mustard together, then add the two oils, sugar, and salt and pepper to taste. A liquidiser is not essential, but it does produce a superb liaison.

Pour the mixture on top of the garlic, screw on the lid, and keep the vinaigrette in a cool place, but not the refrigerator, until needed, for up to two days. Shake well before use.

Mayonnaise

This is a basic mayonnaise, but you can easily vary its colour and flavour. Add garlic for aïoli, basil for a fresh green mayonnaise. The rouille that enhances Provençal fish soups is based on mayonnaise (see below).

Serves 6

2 very fresh, organic egg yolks
1 tsp Dijon mustard
salt and white pepper

300ml (10fl oz) sunflower oil
juice of ½ lemon

Put the egg yolks with the mustard and a pinch of salt in a medium ceramic or glass bowl. Whisk until well mixed, then add the olive oil drop by drop, whisking all the time. When the mixture starts to thicken – which means the oil is being absorbed by the egg yolks – you can pour the oil in a little faster, in a thin, steady stream. But be careful not to go too quickly, otherwise the emulsion will separate.

When all the oil is has been incorporated, add salt and pepper to taste and beat in the lemon juice. Use straight away or keep chilled for two to three days.

Rouille Make the mayo as above, but using 2 tsp Dijon mustard and omitting the lemon juice. At the end, when all the oil is incorporated, stir in two very finely chopped garlic cloves (almost puréed, in fact), ½ tsp cayenne pepper, and 1 tsp paprika.
Basil Mayonnaise Purée a large bunch of basil with 1 tbsp hot water, and stir into the mayonnaise.

Fresh Herb Pesto

This is a pesto made using a selection of herbs, but of course the recipe can be adapted and you could use one herb only: basil for the traditional pesto from Genoa, or flat-leaf parsley for a different flavour.

Serves 4

100g (3½oz) mixed herb leaves
    (thyme, chives, basil, flat-leaf parsley,
    a little sage, coriander)
1 garlic clove, chopped
1 tsp coarse sea salt

30g (1oz) pine nuts
50g (1¾oz) Parmesan cheese,
    freshly grated
200ml (7fl oz) extra virgin olive oil

Put the herbs and garlic in a small blender with the sea salt, and chop well. Now add the pine nuts, and blend again. Stir in the Parmesan, then slowly add the olive oil, stirring well as you do so. Taste for seasoning, and adjust as needed. Keep for only a day or so – it's best fresh.

Warm Yellow and Red Pepper Salsa

I love the idea of fresh and warm vegetable sauces, and this one goes perfectly with the little cheese soufflés on p.25. In fact, this colourful salsa with its slight kick of chilli would go well with chicken, fish and vegetables too.

Serves 4

2 shallots, diced
2 tbsp olive oil
1 yellow pepper, deseeded and finely diced
1 red pepper, deseeded and finely diced

1 small green chilli, deseeded and finely
    diced
salt and pepper
1 tbsp finely chopped flat-leaf parsley

In a large frying pan over a medium heat, soften the shallot in the olive oil without browning for 2 minutes. Now add the yellow and red peppers and the chilli, and sweat for a further 4 minutes until soft.

Season with salt and pepper, and fold in the parsley. Serve the sauce warm as an accompaniment (although it's good cold, too).

Piquant Tomato Sauce

This sauce is very piquant in flavour, and tastes very oriental, mainly due to the cumin and cardamom seeds, and the hoisin sauce. It's not for pasta, therefore, but it's good with the stuffed poussins on pp.78–79, and with other roasted birds and meats.

Serves 4–6

4 garlic cloves, finely chopped
2 onions, finely chopped
1cm (½in) piece of fresh root ginger, finely crushed
1 red chilli, deseeded and finely chopped
2 tbsp olive oil
1 tsp cumin seeds

1 rounded tbsp green cardamon pods, bashed a bit to release the seeds
8 very ripe large tomatoes, chopped
350ml (12fl oz) Chicken Stock (p.206) or Vegetable Stock (p.208)
2 tbsp hoisin or plum sauce
salt and pepper

In a large heavy frying pan, soften the garlic, onion, ginger and chilli in the oil; do not allow to brown. Add the cumin and cardamon pods, mix well, and cook for a few minutes until fragrant. Add the chopped tomatoes, stock and hoisin or plum sauce, and continue stirring for a further 20 minutes or until the sauce thickens. Push through a fine sieve, and season to taste with salt and pepper. If the sauce is too thick, add a little more stock to make it the right consistency. Keep to one side until required, for up to four days, in the refrigerator.

Fresh Mango Pickle

A fresh pickle, which could go with your curry, as a mango chutney would, but it's much more versatile than that. I think it's great for a barbecue, going well as a side salad with chicken, lamb, or fish, or it enhances cold meats fantastically. It will last a few days in the refrigerator – if you can resist it.

Serves 6

2 shallots, peeled and finely chopped
1 small red pepper, skinned (p.23), deseeded and diced
1 tbsp olive oil
2 ripe mangoes, skinned, stoned, and diced
1 red chilli pepper, deseeded and finely sliced

finely grated rind and juice of 2 limes
2 large tomatoes, skinned (p.146), deseeded, and diced
about 2 tbsp chopped flat-leaf parsley
1 tbsp chopped coriander leaves (optional)
1 tsp caster sugar
salt and pepper

Soften the shallot and red pepper in the oil for about 3 minutes on a low heat. Then strain well. Mix all the ingredients together in a dish, and leave in the refrigerator to marinate.

Bring the pickle to room temperature before serving.

Index

London, New York, Munich, Melbourne, Delhi

For Dorling Kindersley
Senior Editor Peter Jones
Senior Art Editor Sara Robin
Executive Managing Editor Adèle Hayward
Managing Art Editor Kat Mead
Art Director Peter Luff
Publisher Stephanie Jackson
Senior Production Editor Jenny Woodcock
Senior Production Controller Wendy Penn
Creative Technical Support Sonia Charbonnier

Produced for Dorling Kindersley by
Editor Susan Fleming
Designer Caz Hildebrand (www.heredesign.co.uk)
Photography Lis Parsons

First published in Great Britain in 2008 by Dorling Kindersley Limited
80 Strand, London WC2R 0RL

A Penguin Company
2 4 6 8 10 9 7 5 3 1

Copyright © 2008 Dorling Kindersley Limited, London
Text copyright © Rosemary Shrager

A CIP catalogue record for this book is available from
The British Library
ISBN 978-1-4053-3513-3

Printed by Mohn in Germany.
Reproduction by MDP, Bath, UK

See our complete catalogue at www.dk.com

Acknowledgements

The author would like to thank the following people:
Susan Fleming for her patience. All the people at Dorling Kindersley
– Stephanie Jackson who had so much enthusiasm and belief in me,
Peter Jones for his never-ending calmness which got me through,
Sara Robin, Kat Mead, Peter Luff, and Adèle Hayward. Also a
special thank you to Caz Hildebrand the designer and Lis Parsons
the photographer.

Heather Holden-Brown my very patient agent and old school friend,
and my wonderful TV agent Anne Kibel. Sam Squire for her sense of
humour and professionalism. Sue Mountgarret who helps me design
my courses at Swinton Park and test recipes, Lyn Carter who helped
me with my recipes in the past, and Angela Maw who keeps my
work in order. Gilly who has been my amazing hardworking
assistant for five years and keeps me in order, and my family who
have been the most amazing support.

RDF Media and RDF West, Grant Mansfield, Mark Hill and
Amanda Fidler who made a really fabulous programme, and also a
big thank you to Ali Sharman and Adam MacDonald from ITV who
believed in the series and made it happen. I would like to specially
thank the wonderful film crew for their endless hard work and
dedication, and for singing with me every morning.

Some local shops: the butchers W. S. Rogers & Son, Beavers
Butchers, all the other food shops in Masham, Carricks Fish, Snape,
and R & J Butchers, Kirby Melstead.

Susan Cunliffe-Lister for her support and all those wonderful
vegetables and fruit she produces every year at Swinton Park, and
Mark and Felicity Cunliffe-Lister and everybody at Swinton Park for
all their support throughout the year.

DK would like to thank:
Mark Lesbirel and all at RDF, Rebekah Lord at ITV, Mark and Felicity
Cunliffe-Lister and all at Swinton Park.
Louise Coe, Daniel Mills and Siobhan O'Connor for editorial
assistance. Natasha Montgomery and Katherine Raj for invaluable
design assistance.
Emma-Jane Frost for assisting with food styling, Rachel Jukes for
prop styling, Claire Tennant-Scull for proofreading and Margaret
McCormack for the index.

All location photography was taken at:
Swinton Park, Masham, Ripon, North Yorkshire, HG4 4JH
T: (01765) 680900 F: (01765) 680901
enquiries@swintonpark.com, www.swintonpark.com SWINTON PARK